D0006070

Is the gospel that unites us more powerful t[...]
do you start Christians in a conversation [...]
America? In this brief book, Isaac Adams g[...]
begin the journey. Adams points us to lister[...]
with prayer—as the place to start. He's right. This book will lower defenses
and encourage love. I pray that God gives this book a great ministry among
us, displaying the division-overcoming power of the gospel.

MARK DEVER, pastor, Capitol Hill Baptist
Church, and president of 9Marks.org

This is one of the most insightful, wise-for-the-times books I have read.
It is so deeply needed, and I will be recommending it widely. My only
regret was that it didn't come out sooner. I almost wept thinking about
the thousands of churches that could have used this book in the summer
of 2020—the summer of George Floyd. But I rejoice thinking of how
many people will read it now. There are millions of people who need to
read this book.

MICHAEL O. EMERSON, professor of sociology, University
of Illinois Chicago, coauthor, *Divided by Faith:
Evangelical Religion and the Problem of Race in America*

Making progress in racial reconciliation is one of the most pressing needs
of the church today, and we desperately need gospel-centered, culturally adept, clear-eyed, humility-rich, biblically wise, prayer-soaked,
unflinching-yet-gracious guidance in it. Isaac's book asks some great
questions and offers much needed insight into both the biblical and cultural dimensions of these questions. I have come to love and trust Isaac's
counsel in many areas, and in this book he is at his best.

J. D. GREEAR, pastor, The Summit Church,
Raleigh-Durham, North Carolina

Race and racism can seem like abstract topics. Everyone has an opinion.
It's easy to share our opinions in the abstract. But how do we actually talk
to each other about it, especially among fellow believers? That's what sets
this book apart. As an African-American pastor in multiethnic settings,

Isaac Adams knows how these conversations go well and where they go wrong. This is the book we need for relevant advice not only on how to think about an "issue" but how to listen, learn, and love.

MICHAEL HORTON, professor of theology, Westminster
Seminary California and host of the White Horse Inn

It's easy to pretend that the American church doesn't have a problem with race; it's even easier, when you see the problem, to despair. What's hard is to look our sins right in the face and still bring a message of gospel hope. That's what Isaac Adams does in this sober and strong, wise and practical book. May we all have ears to hear.

ALAN JACOBS, distinguished professor of humanities,
Baylor University, and senior fellow, the Institute for
Advanced Studies in Culture, University of Virginia

With clarity and insight, courage and compassion, Isaac Adams has provided an elixir of a book for Christians who are weary and worn out by the effects of the poison that often accompanies conversations on race and justice. Using realistic stories and Scripture to both illuminate the mind and stir the heart, he reveals the importance of learning how to lament and listen so as to more effectively learn and love the "other," whoever that may be. His insights are realistic without being simplistic, pragmatic without being dogmatic. So, for anyone wishing to learn how to better navigate the challenging conversations regarding racial reconciliation, this book is a must-read.

JULIUS J. KIM, PhD, president, The Gospel Coalition

Books and articles on race typically make an argument or offer a perspective, which are good things to do. Yet this book feels different. Isaac writes as a pastor who, more than anything, loves his sheep—Black and White, Asian and Hispanic—and wants to do them good. He wants them to love and to know love. I've not read anything else like it on the topic.

JONATHAN LEEMAN, editorial director, 9Marks.org, and author of
How the Nations Rage: Rethinking Faith and Politics in a Divided Age

Isaac Adams's powerful new book is an invaluable resource for individuals and churches who want to get better at talking about race. Its innovative format helps us all to empathize with other people's hopes and fears, and to get why conversations can become so fraught so fast. If you're looking for a prayer-soaked, Jesus-honoring, biblically grounded kick start to better conversations about race, this book is for you.

Dr. Rebecca McLaughlin, author of *Confronting Christianity*, *10 Questions Every Teen Should Ask (and Answer) about Christianity*, and *The Secular Creed*

Sadly, Christian conversations about race and justice in the United States have been hijacked. Some radicalize the discussion, while others politicize it. Either way, the result has been a divided church. If you are grieved by the fracture between Christians in our churches and our culture, you'll want to read *Talking about Race*. Adams equips us to have the hard conversations by helping us understand the present vocabulary, allowing us to listen to the voices of diverse brothers and sisters, and pointing us back to the gospel of Christ and the Christ of the gospel—our only hope. So, my dear brothers and sisters, I appeal to you. Let's stop assuming the worst about each other, and let's start talking.

Juan R. Sanchez, senior pastor, High Pointe Baptist Church, Austin, Texas

Through *Talking about Race*, Isaac Adams calls us to navigate the race conversation as Christians in America. With gentleness, wisdom, and pastoral care, Adams will make you think more deeply about your own personal convictions, stereotypes, and biases that typically go unchallenged or unspoken. Whether or not you agree with every detail, you'll walk away having gained compassion and empathy for others and be equipped with biblical guidance and practical steps for how to move forward. I'm thankful for this helpful book.

Laura Wifler, author, podcaster, and cofounder of Risen Motherhood

Isaac Adams has written a clear, conversational, and accessible book to help Christians talk about race. Even when readers disagree with Adams's prose, analysis, and suggestions, they will still learn from the fruit of his labor.

JARVIS J. WILLIAMS, associate professor of New
Testament Interpretation, The Southern Baptist
Theological Seminary, Louisville, Kentucky

When I wrote *Beyond Racial Gridlock*, I was asked to also provide a companion book to help Christians with this conversation. At that time, I wished I had written *Talking about Race*. This is the book I have been praying for. It challenges all of us how to speak to each other as believers who are struggling to discuss these sensitive issues. Adams provides guidance to help us navigate the minefields that confront our racial conversations. This book is a critical missing piece for the development of real Christian racial reconciliation. If you want to gain practical insight into how to apply our Christian principles to our racial conversations, then pick up this book.

GEORGE YANCEY, professor, the Institute for
Studies of Religion, Baylor University

TALKING
ABOUT RACE

*Gospel
Hope for Hard
Conversations*

ISAAC
ADAMS

ZONDERVAN
REFLECTIVE

ZONDERVAN REFLECTIVE

Talking about Race
Copyright © 2022 by Isaac Adams

Requests for information should be addressed to:
Zondervan, *3900 Sparks Dr. SE, Grand Rapids, Michigan 49546*

Zondervan titles may be purchased in bulk for educational, business, fundraising, or sales promotional use. For information, please email SpecialMarkets@Zondervan.com.

ISBN 978-0-310-12442-9 (softcover)
ISBN 978-0-310-12443-6 (ebook)
ISBN 978-0-310-12444-3 (audio)
ISBN 978-0-310-63729-5 (custom)

All Scripture quotations, unless otherwise indicated, are taken from the ESV® Bible (The Holy Bible, English Standard Version®). Copyright © 2001 by Crossway, a publishing ministry of Good News Publishers. Used by permission. All rights reserved.

Scripture quotations marked NASB are taken from the New American Standard Bible®. Copyright © 1960, 1962, 1963, 1968, 1971, 1972, 1973, 1975, 1977, 1995 by The Lockman Foundation. Used by permission. (www.Lockman.org).

Scripture quotations marked NIV are taken from The Holy Bible, New International Version®, NIV®. Copyright © 1973, 1978, 1984, 2011 by Biblica, Inc.® Used by permission of Zondervan. All rights reserved worldwide. www.Zondervan.com. The "NIV" and "New International Version" are trademarks registered in the United States Patent and Trademark Office by Biblica, Inc.®

Any internet addresses (websites, blogs, etc.) and telephone numbers in this book are offered as a resource. They are not intended in any way to be or imply an endorsement by Zondervan, nor does Zondervan vouch for the content of these sites and numbers for the life of this book.

All rights reserved. No part of this publication may be reproduced, stored in a retrieval system, or transmitted in any form or by any means—electronic, mechanical, photocopy, recording, or any other—except for brief quotations in printed reviews, without the prior permission of the publisher.

Cover design: Micah Kandros Design
Cover art: © *MicroOne / Shutterstock*
Interior design: Denise Froehlich

Printed in the United States of America

22 23 24 25 26   /LSC/   10 9 8 7 6 5 4 3 2 1

For Jan Adams, my mother,
who taught me that a mind is a terrible thing to waste.
I am rising up and calling you blessed.

"I am a man of unclean lips, and I dwell in the midst of a people of unclean lips."

—ISAIAH 6:5

We wear the mask that grins and lies,
It hides our cheeks and shades our eyes,—
This debt we pay to human guile;
With torn and bleeding hearts we smile,
And mouth with myriad subtleties.

Why should the world be over-wise,
In counting all our tears and sighs?
Nay, let them only see us, while
 We wear the mask.

We smile, but, O great Christ, our cries
To thee from tortured souls arise.
We sing, but oh the clay is vile
Beneath our feet, and long the mile;
But let the world dream otherwise,
 We wear the mask!

—PAUL LAURENCE DUNBAR (1896)[1]

CONTENTS

WHY I WROTE THIS BOOK

May the God of hope fill you with all joy and peace in believing, so that by the power of the Holy Spirit you may abound in hope.

—ROMANS 15:13

But have opponents of mass incarceration done their job by simply describing and detailing the phenomenon? Have public advocates rendered their best service to communities by refusing to point a way forward? Has it compounded the problem by leaving off solutions? Have our best public intellectuals been the best public servants, if they convey no hope?

—THABITI ANYABWILE[1]

"If I can be honest with you," I said to my congregation, "even as I prepared to give this talk, I was shaking in my boots."

So began a lecture that was the seed of this book—a book I did not intend to write. Originally, I set out to write a different book. It would have been a book giving biblical and practical guidance on where Christians could begin to combat racism. I wanted to help evangelicals (generally) and white evangelicals (specifically) who were sincerely sympathetic to racial concerns but at a loss about how to respond to them. I sought to answer *the* question they ask me when I teach on race and racism: "What can I do?"

But then, as I began preparing that book, Ahmaud Arbery was gunned down. And in the wake of this tragedy, African American actor Sterling K. Brown went live on Facebook after returning from a particularly hard run.[2] (If you are familiar with Arbery's case, you know why it was pertinent for Brown to speak after going for a run.) While running is inherently challenging, what made this run especially hard for Brown was the facemask he had to wear; such garb had become standard during the COVID-19 outbreak. The mask stifled Brown's breath. The mask obscured Brown's face. And there was even more to his mask than met the eye.

Brown testified of how, as a black man who regularly navigates white spaces, he always had to wear a mask of sorts, albeit invisible. Brown echoed the same struggle poet Paul Laurence Dunbar described over a hundred years earlier in his poem "We Wear the Mask." Like many black people in predominantly white spaces, Dunbar and Brown didn't feel safe to be honest about who they were or what they experienced.

And I couldn't shake the thought of that hiding.

Brown's video haunted me. It resonated with me on many levels. As a black man in twenty-first-century America lamenting yet another racial tragedy. As a father of three precious brown babies. As a pastor of a church that is multiethnic in one sense, predominantly white in another sense—a church that sits in Washington, DC. Chocolate city. My hometown.

You see, as a pastor shepherding people from lots of different ethnicities, I knew people who felt like Brown. Regardless of their racial background, not a few of them felt like they had to wear a mask when talking about race. Yet they didn't realize they were wearing these masks and that others were too. I kept thinking about this dilemma, and it occurred to me that before we could talk about *action*, we would be helped to talk to one another—period—and learn why we struggled to do even that. That is, before we answer the question "What can I do?" we'd be helped to answer questions like "Why am I hiding?" "At what cost am I hiding?" "Why are others around me hiding?" "Why do I not realize they are hiding?"

If we could answer these questions, I thought, we would have a better understanding of the very problems we so desperately wanted to address. If we could answer these questions, we would be better suited to combat the racism we Christians say we hate and maintain the unity so many of us say we want. I felt, and still do, that it is imperative to bring biblical light to the "why" of Christians' dysfunctional communications about race. If we could do this, we would not agree on every racial detail (at least not in this life). But maybe we could see that *it is possible* to hold our beliefs *and* hold our tongues, or at least employ them in better ways. If we could do this, one of the hardest challenges for churches in America—loving across racial lines—could become one of their most powerful testimonies to a divided and dividing world. If we could think about our communication challenges regarding race, by God's grace, we could show the world a different world.

In summary, if we better appreciate the difficulty of conversations about race, we will better appreciate one another. We will be slower to grow angry, quicker to confess, and quicker to forgive. It is popular nowadays to highlight the problems of God's people when it comes to race, and indeed, if one is looking for fault, people can find it. No doubt, God's people are a mess, *but* we are a beloved mess. And despite our mess, I believe God still equips us with the tools to take up conversations about race in a uniquely powerful and needed way. It's high time we got to work.

And so the original idea for my book changed, and I tried to write a book to the ends I described above. I aimed to write a book pastors could hand to their people without having to make ten qualifications. I sought to write a book that didn't just name the problem but also charted a biblical way forward. I wanted the book to burst with stories because stories are powerful. Stories stick, just ask Nathan the prophet and David the king (see 2 Samuel 12). Most of all, however, I wanted to write a book that exalted the Lord Jesus Christ. He is our greatest need for the present hour and for every hour. He always will be.

This book isn't a systematic theology on race nor an exhaustive history of American racism. What's more, this isn't a perfect book. But perfection isn't my goal; faithfulness is. And I rest happily knowing that though I didn't do things perfectly, I did something a lot of people in this conversation haven't done—I tried. I tried my best. That, it seems, is all we can do.

Romans 11:36
Isaac Adams

INTRODUCTION

Let each one of you speak the truth with his neighbor.

—EPHESIANS 4:25

If one thing is clear about the American public discourse today, it's that we're totally ill-equipped or unwilling to engage in honest debate. This makes solving issues such as police reform and racial injustices very difficult.

—JUSTIN GIBONEY[1]

"Why is it so hard for Christians in America to talk about race with each other?" Have you ever asked a question like that? Why is there so much defensiveness and division, suspicion and strife on racial matters among those who claim to be united in Jesus? Christians expect difficulty with the world; Jesus promised it in John 16:33. And sure, opponents do also arise from *within* the church, and this presents its own trouble (Acts 20:30). That said, churches are fundamentally families, aren't they? Should talking about race with brothers and sisters in the faith be so hard?

After all, aren't Christians supposed to be quick to listen, slow to speak, and slow to anger (James 1:19)? Aren't we to be truth-in-love speakers (Ephesians 4:15) and burden bearers (Galatians 6:2)?

Can't the gospel overcome any barrier, including ethnic divides (Ephesians 2:11–22)? If so, why is it so hard for us to speak with grace *and* truth about issues of race?

As we'll soon see, the answers are manifold. Suffice it to say for now though, just like in the world, there is broken trust between ethnicities in many American evangelical churches. We see it on social media. We hear it in conversations (or the lack thereof).

It seems that every season a new but eerily familiar, racially charged tragedy goes viral. When it does, we know what will happen: many *Christians* will take polar-opposite sides; others will feel torn, confused, and disheartened in the middle. Whether fights and quarrels break out or one side is met with deafening silence, not a few people will get incensed. Old wounds will fester. Bad memories will haunt us anew. Long-standing resentment will boil up. Friendships will end. Amid various manifestations of racism's painful legacy in this land, hearts will harden as believers feel betrayed and skeptical of each other's sincerity, love, and faithfulness to the Lord.

Among the responses to these racial challenges, one is all too common: American evangelicals shy away from speaking honestly about our divides—especially across color lines. We struggle to discuss racial matters with others outside our own ethnicity. Even if members of different ethnicities sit in the same churches, too often we wear masks, metaphorically speaking, to avoid one of our greatest difficulties: sharing with each other what we truthfully think about race and racism. Indeed, this is something too many of us feel we simply cannot do. We may feel that way because of apathy, fear, ignorance, exhaustion, or some mix of all these factors. We may feel that way out of a sincere desire to "maintain the unity of the Spirit in the bond of peace" (Ephesians 4:3). Whatever our reason, we hide from each other. In so doing, we hinder genuine love, which bears witness to a watching world about Jesus and the authenticity of our following him. "By this all people will know that you are my disciples, if you have love for one another" (John 13:35).

But what if Christians, by God's grace, could honestly reckon with race and have positive conversations with one another that cause us to grow together in love rather than apart in bitterness? What if each member of our churches felt they could be honest about race *and* still be loved by their brothers and sisters at church? What might happen to our witness, our churches, our neighborhoods, and ourselves if we stopped trying to save face, grinning and bearing the pain? In other words—what might happen if we dropped our masks?

The aim of this book is twofold. First, this book aims to help us *think*, in light of God's Word, about why conversations regarding race and racism are so hard—yet also so important—for Christians in America. Second, this book aims to help us *think* about how we can have these conversations more helpfully. If both aims are accomplished, by God's grace, we'll be better equipped to faithfully pursue that which we supposedly desire regarding race relations. Want to keep doing justice to your neighbor? Then you should think about this conversational struggle. Want to be better prepared to maintain authentic, God-glorifying, multiethnic fellowship in your church? Then you should think about this conversational struggle. Indeed, understanding the communication breakdown across racial divides, and the damage that results from it, is not only important for following Jesus amid race relations—it's foundational. After all, if we can't even talk with one another, what hope do we have for loving each other, much less our neighbors?

We'll explore questions like these from a hopeful and pastoral perspective. By hopeful, I mean I'll write as if Jesus is alive and well, and in charge too. By pastoral, I mean I'll talk with you as if you're my friend, not my enemy, for "the Lord's servant must not be quarrelsome but kind to everyone" (2 Timothy 2:24).

We'll revisit this pastoral emphasis soon, but let me first clarify who the "you" in that last sentence is. Who is my audience? I'm writing to Christians. Not anyone who simply identifies as a

Christian—maybe as a loose cultural affiliation. Rather, I'm writing to Christians who treasure their Bibles, exalt their Savior, cherish the gospel, repent of their sins, seek their sanctification, and love their church. And I'm writing to a wide swath of those Christians. To white Christians who aren't sure how to pursue racial reconciliation (or whether that's even the right term to use). To black Christians who are tired of receiving white Christians' indifference, ignorance, or scorn. To Hispanic and Asian Christians who'd like to talk about more than the black-white dynamic. To pastors trying to navigate all these waters.

Christian, if you're frustrated with the racial status quo, I'm writing to you. If you're considering leaving your church for another because of disagreements about race, I'm writing to you. If you feel like you can't talk honestly about race with others, I have news for you: you're not alone.

What This Book Is and Isn't Saying

A good relationship is one in which you don't have to make a bunch of disclaimers, but I recognize that you and I don't know each other, hence this section. In this book, I intend to focus on saying something rather than defending what I'm not saying. But given how easily people can be misread in conversations about race, I want to clarify what I am and am not saying. So here are four disclaimers.

First, I'm writing to and about Christians in America, not because America is exceptional in God's sight (it's not), but because that's the context I know and in which I've pastored. While America has problems in common with the rest of the world (e.g., sin), we also have our own unique racial problems and history to think about.

Second, I am suggesting that one major problem is that a lot of Christians don't feel they can honestly speak about race issues. But I am not suggesting that's our only problem. I say this because some might retort that the problem is *not* just that Christians do not feel they can be honest; after all, plenty of Christians are sharing what they honestly think. Rather, the problem is what some of us *honestly believe.* As Jesus said, out of the abundance of the heart the mouth speaks (Luke 6:45). I sympathize with this retort. Yet if no one is listening to what another says, how do we expect to get to the issues of the heart? Further, I believe that addressing issues of the mouth can helpfully highlight problems of the heart. Finally, not all beliefs will be or need to be changed. Still, we need to learn how to live with and love one another, don't we? And so we're giving the matter of honest conversation serious thought.

Third, I'm suggesting that Christians in America have a problem when it comes to talking about race and racism. But I'm not suggesting that this is our worst problem. I'm not suggesting that our bickering is the real problem rather than the injustices we're bickering about. I'm not saying that everything would be fine if we just didn't argue. And I make this point because Martin Luther King Jr. was right—too many of us look only for the absence of tension but not the presence of justice, and this makes for negative peace.[2] That said, I believe we will understand the problem of racial injustice better if we understand why we can't talk with one another. Paying attention to the symptoms may teach us something about the disease. Put differently, rightly studying the smaller problem of racial communication can help us understand the larger problem of racial strife that has for so long split our churches, communities, and nation. What's more, if we hold up this smaller problem to the light of God's Word, maybe—just maybe—we won't only gain insight about the larger problem of racial strife but also hope for how we might faithfully follow Jesus within the strife.

Fourth and finally, in light of that last point, I'm suggesting that we need more honest conversations about race across color lines. But I'm not suggesting that conversations are all we need. Some folks will rightly wonder what good will come from more conversations. "We've been talking for years, haven't we? We've had our racial-reconciliation conferences. We've heard the panels. It's new laws we need!" I sympathize with this point, but a lot of people are still showing up to this conversation brand-new. This book is meant to help them, which is to say that this book is a starting point—not a finish line.

Moreover, the polarization of the day is so bad that while many of us may have already talked about talking, fresh attention to the dysfunctional communication across ethnic lines is more than warranted. My friend said this about America after the 2020 presidential election between Donald Trump and Joe Biden: "We are living in two different countries, each falling further into our echo chambers, believing we are the only ones with access to the true, the good, and the beautiful. Each believing we are in the vast majority. Well, neither of us are. If we want to heal, we need to understand those we hate. It starts with asking two questions. First, what are the things I could be wrong about? And second, what motivates others to believe differently than I do?"

May God give us grace to listen to the answers.

What This Book Is Saying	What This Book Isn't Saying
Christians in America have a communication problem regarding race and racism that's worth studying in light of God's Word.	• This communication problem is our *only* problem. • This communication problem is our *worst* problem. • All we need to do is talk more to resolve racial injustices.

How This Book Works—as a Workbook

This book is divided into two parts. Part 1 will prepare us for the questions posed in part 2 by helping us to identify the masks we and others wear. It will help us feel the weight of our communication problems. In part 1 we'll meet fictional characters who represent a broad range of people, just as many churches have a wide range of folks in their membership. Their names are Hunter, Darius, Anna Beth, Samantha Lee, Jane, and Pastor Bruce. They live in or around Philadelphia, and they're all members of the same predominantly white church—Lincoln Ridge Bible Church (LRBC). All the characters are hearing national news that just broke: an unarmed, black image bearer was gunned down by police in Chicago. How will our friends respond? And what will be the responses of their family, networks, and church?

Over the course of the first five chapters, we'll see each character's vantage point on this news. Following each character's scene are questions. Don't skip them. Answer them. In a journal. On a note in your phone. Wherever you answer them, just answer them, even if you're reading this book by yourself. This is a short book that requires long work; that is, it works best as a workbook. I'm not asking you to do anything I won't do myself. After you answer the first set of questions, I'll offer my commentary on the character's story and highlight lessons we could learn from it. I call my commentaries "encouragements" because they express the encouragements I would offer to each character as if I were counseling them as their pastor. I won't resolve (or even touch on) every issue raised in each character's story, as no difficult counseling case can be resolved in one session, but I'll touch on key issues for our communication across ethnic lines.

Through the stories and questions, my hope is that you will see how the characters wear different masks for different reasons, depending on whether they come from the minority or majority culture.[3] They don't all wear their masks for equally good reasons or with equal difficulty, but they wear them nonetheless. Of course these fictitious friends don't represent every experience, but they do represent common ones—experiences I hear of often as a pastor.

In part 2 we'll answer basic questions many Christians in America are asking right now. Questions like, Why should we talk about race across color lines? Why is it so hard to do so? And how should we do it?

A Pastoral Perspective

In this book, I try to speak pastorally, as I'm primarily writing this book as a pastor—not as a sociologist, psychologist, or historian (though I'm thankful for those who have given their life's work to these disciplines). One thing my writing from a pastoral perspective means is that you won't find a lot of statistics in this book. And that's because, as a pastor, though I am trying to address the mind, I'm also trying to address *the heart and soul* of the matter, not the data of it per se (Matthew 22:37). To be clear, data *can* reveal the mind, heart, and soul, but it doesn't always or completely do so. Moreover, I've been in enough conversations about race to know that everyone has their set of stats that allows them to remain within their predetermined camp. So, stats can be true, but stats are also necessarily disputable and mutable. Is the glass 50 percent full or 50 percent empty? The truth is, it's both—but it depends on who you ask.

All of this to say, stats shift; God's Word doesn't. And as a pastor, I'm going to have that unchanging Word be the lamp for our feet and the light for our path as we journey through this book. To be sure, that doesn't mean that everything I'll say is necessarily mandated by Scripture, and that makes sense, since there is not a straight line from the Bible to every issue I'll raise. I'll at times give counsel that falls more in the realm of prudence than prescription, and godly Christians may disagree with me, and that's fine. While I pray my counsel challenges you, my main concern is not *that* you disagree but *how* you disagree. And I pray that as we think together about how we do and don't speak about race, we'll find ourselves and our churches being able to lower our masks, even as we read about others raising theirs.

One Last Note

I've emphasized the difficulty of talking about race *with someone of another ethnicity*. That's because if we talk about race, we might feel okay doing so with family and friends who talk like us or share our political sympathies. But that's just it—we *trust* those people. And generally, the boundaries for who *those people* are in our circles fall along ethnic (or color) lines. Inside the lines, we are confident those people will be nice to us. Inside the lines, we are confident they'll give our sincere questions and qualms a fair hearing. Do you have this level of confidence in your fellow church members, especially across color lines? Do they have this confidence in you? Why or why not?

Please answer the questions.

Questions for Reflection and Discussion

1. Read Ephesians 4:17–32 aloud and pray. What does this passage mean for your conversations about race? In what ways have you not lived up to it? In what ways have you lived up to it by God's grace? Ask a friend you disagree with on racial issues how they think you've done in these conversations (and assure them you won't respond with sinful anger).

2. The introduction claimed, "Just like in the world, there is broken trust between ethnicities in many American churches." Ever since Adam and Eve sinned in the garden, God's people have been tempted to be like the world. When it comes to race and racism, how have American evangelicals given in to this temptation? How have they fought it?

3. Do you think there's broken trust between ethnicities in your church and city? Is your congregation one in which you can have honest conversations about race? Why or why not?

4. I'm speaking primarily to and about evangelicals in America. However, while America has its own racial history, racism is not unique to America. What international examples of racial strife can you think of? What lessons do these examples provide?

PART

1

If you bite and devour each other, watch out or you will be destroyed by each other.

—GALATIANS 5:15 NIV

Walk and talk in the manner of love, for God is love.

—COMMANDMENT 3 OF MARTIN LUTHER KING
JR.'S PLEDGE FOR VOLUNTEERS[1]

SETTING THE SCENE

A Tragic Shooting, a Viral Video

Let love be genuine. Abhor what is evil.

—ROMANS 12:9

The problem of the twentieth century is the problem of the color-line.

—W. E. B. DU BOIS[1]

He was just a fifth grader, but already Jackson Lowry had a different Monday than most kids in the country, or at least it felt that way. He'd been cast into a political contest at his Christian school, Lincoln Ridge Christian Academy. LRCA was founded in the 1960s by white families who had moved to the suburbs so they could get out of the city. However, in the last couple decades the neighborhood had changed—to some parents' chagrin. The school was now a fairly diverse place. There were lots of black kids like Jackson, lots of white kids like his best friend, Clay Caulkins, and that wasn't the half of it. Everyone seemed to get along great—that is, until one of Jackson's classmates had put up that sheet of paper on their classroom door.

"Who Are You Voting For?" the page was titled. There were two choices: the Democrat presidential candidate atop the left-hand column and the Republican candidate atop the right. Most of Jackson's ten-year-old classmates had filled in their names in one of the columns to pronounce who they (that is, their parents) were voting for. They'd then gone outside to play.

Jackson, one of the last students in the room, was tying his shoes, about to head out, when he stopped to steal a look at his newly decorated classroom door. He didn't know much about presidents or elections. But looking at the sheet, he did notice most of the names on the left were his black friends, and most of the names on the right were his white ones.

Jackson's attention broke away from the divided list when he heard his friend Clay shout, "Watch out!" Had Jackson waited two more seconds to duck, he would have been nailed in the head by the basketball Clay had thrown at him.

"Almost got you, dude. What are you staring at anyway, Jax?" Clay asked his friend and teammate.

"Oh, uh, just this voting list on the door," Jackson answered.

"Ah, yeah, I need to sign that. My dad likes this guy," Clay said pointing his finger at the right-hand side. Jackson wasn't surprised. "Let's sign it after recess, though. C'mon!" Clay said, inviting Jackson to do what they always did at this time—have fun together.

The boys started out the door. For whatever reason, Jackson felt relieved he didn't have to sign the paper in front of Clay, if at all. As they were running, Clay stopped Jackson. *Oh no*, Jackson thought to himself, worried Clay would want to turn back around and register their vote.

"Hey, why didn't you come to my birthday party on Saturday?" Clay asked Jackson. "My dad rented paintball guns, and we all played with them in my backyard!"

Jackson had to think quickly. For some reason he couldn't describe, he didn't feel like he could explain his absence to Clay.

Honestly, he couldn't even explain it to himself. Jackson just knew that his dad was real worked up about the thought of him going to Clay's birthday party.

"No. No. No way, Son," Jackson's dad had said to him. "You ain't going to play with some toy guns in a white neighborhood. It's not safe. Period. End of discussion."

"I got sick," Jackson told Clay, lying to his friend. "I barfed that afternoon, right before your party."

"Really?!" Clay asked, his eyes opening wide. "That's gross! And awesome! What color was it?"

"Uh, well—" Jackson was about to make up some answer to further this fable when he was interrupted by a gasp. The boys heard their teacher crying. They peeked back into the classroom to see what the matter was.

"Ms. Mack! Ms. Mack! What's wrong?" they asked, running back inside.

"Boys!" she said through a tear-soaked tissue as she, with great hurry, flipped over her phone to hide the screen from her unexpected visitors. "I'm okay. You should be outside."

"You sure, Ms. Mack?" Clay asked.

"Yes. Thank you, but please go," she said.

"But—" Jackson started.

"Go!" Ms. Mack said, pointing to the door, which she hadn't realized had become a voting booth.

Confused, the boys started again out the door but hid in the hallway near their classroom. Ms. Mack sat at her desk, turned her phone back over, and resumed the news anchor's horrible report:

Malachi Brewers, a twenty-two-year-old black man, was gunned down by police on Monday afternoon at approximately 2:00 p.m. Brewers, who had just finished his shift delivering pizzas, was in a ShopRite in a Chicago suburb. A white sales associate who had been following Brewers in the store claims he saw Brewers steal a candy bar. The sales associate called after Brewers, and Brewers began to run. The associate chased after Brewers into the parking lot of the strip mall, where an off-duty officer saw Brewers and halted him. Witnesses say they heard Brewers yell, "I don't have nothing! I don't have nothing!" Many understand Brewers to have been attempting to communicate that he didn't have a gun. It is alleged that as he was yelling, Brewers put his hands into his pockets to show the officers a candy bar was all he had. But as he pulled his hands out, four shots rang out. Brewers died at the scene. The situation is live and ongoing, and we'll report back as we know more. For now, you can see the following video of the encounter. Please note: viewer discretion is advised. The content is graphic and disturbing.

Ms. Mack couldn't breathe for a moment. She turned off her phone before the video could play. Assuming all the kids were outside playing, she looked up and saw a curious sheet on her classroom door. She walked over to it.

"Who are you voting for?" she whispered as she read the page through wet eyes. She ripped the paper down, whipped around back into the classroom, and collapsed into her desk chair.

Meanwhile, the boys had heard the reporter's every word.

Questions for Reflection and Discussion

1. What was reading the story of Malachi Brewers like for you?
2. What's your earliest memory of recognizing race and/or racial tension?
3. When conversations about race come up, how do you feel?
4. Why do you think the families who began LRCA wanted to move out of the city?

CHAPTER 2

A MAJORITY MASK—MEET HUNTER

"We do not know what to do."

—2 CHRONICLES 20:12

The most tragic impediment to an honest conversation about race in America is fear—an entirely realistic fear of being slain by the cancel culture. It is impossible to exaggerate the corrupting effect that the terror of being called "racist"—even a whiff of the toxin, the slightest hint, the ghost of an imputation—has on freedom of discussion and the honest workings of the American public mind.

—LANCE MORROW[1]

Six days had passed since Malachi Brewers's death. Or murder. Or killing. Hunter Caulkins didn't know what to call it, but he couldn't spend much time thinking about it. He had to get his family to church. His wife, Julie, and their two daughters were ready to go. Everyone was ready to go. Except one person.

"Clay, come on, buddy! We're going to be late!" Hunter shouted from the bottom of the stairs. He turned to Julie with a look of disbelief and acceptance as he shook his head. "I swear, that kid moves slower than a one-legged turtle."

"Hey," Julie shot back, "he's *your* son." She winked and smiled. Finishing her coffee, she continued watching TV. A news anchor was reporting about what had taken place over the last week—riots. Or protests. Or unrest. Julie didn't know what to call it all, but she didn't spend much time thinking about it before she spoke. "It didn't take long for this to blow up."

"For what to blow up?" Hunter asked. He had his back to the TV as he poured himself a cup of coffee.

"The whole situation with that Brewers guy," she said. "It's really sad."

"Oh yeah. Ugh. Another one of these," Hunter said, looking down. He didn't have much to say, or at least not much desire to say it. He knew he had to tread lightly. Julie, he had learned, was more sympathetic to these events than he was.

"You going to try and talk to Darius about it?" she asked.

Hunter paused for a moment. His mind immediately raced back to the killing of JaVari Dupree—another young black man who was killed by police last summer. Hunter remembered how he and Darius had tried to talk about it. *"Oh, come on, Darius!"* Hunter remembered saying. *"I don't have a racist bone in my body!"* That conversation didn't last long.

Snapping back to the present, Hunter remembered it was Julie he was talking with now, not Darius. "I mean—I want to," Hunter answered his wife. "I—I just don't know what to say. Last time one of these incidents came up, Darius and I just wound up arguing. I swear, every time I open my mouth on this race stuff, I feel like I just step in it," he said before going quiet.

"I get that, but you and Darius have been friends for so long," she answered. "Would it really hurt to try and talk again? We could learn a lot from him. You should find him after the prayer meeting and ask if you can get together sometime this week."

Knowing she couldn't see his face, Hunter rolled his eyes. *That's right,* Hunter thought, *I'm always the student. Darius is always the teacher.* Hunter could feel his blood pressure rising, but he wasn't sure why. He knew he wasn't crazy. After all, he and Darius served as deacons at church with another black guy. *He's even more suspicious about claims of racism than I am,* Hunter thought.

But he didn't say that aloud. He didn't respond further to his wife. He dared not turn his thoughts into speech. Instead, Hunter stared out the window overlooking their backyard. He started to wonder how the prayer meeting would go. It was the first of its kind at Lincoln Ridge Bible Church—an all-church prayer meeting, one that would take place before the regularly scheduled worship service. The pastor had called it to specially pray about Malachi Brewers's case. As a deacon, Hunter needed to be there. As a regular citizen observing the news, Hunter wasn't sure what to think. He was about to dive further into his thoughts when it caught his eyes—his favorite Ginkgo tree, the jewel of Hunter's backyard. The tree greeted his eyes, though a bit more painfully this time, given its fresh coat of neon paintball spray. Thinking of Clay's birthday party, Hunter took a sip of coffee, forgot about Julie pushing him to talk to Darius, and smiled.

Hunter wanted to say more to Julie. He wanted to say how, just like Darius, he loved the Lord. He wanted to say how, like Darius, he hated racism. He wanted to say how he felt for his longtime friend. He wanted to say how the only difference between them was that he was white and Darius was black—and this shouldn't matter that much.

But Hunter didn't feel like he was allowed to say those things, at least not publicly. Even though he and Darius had the same level of education, Hunter felt muzzled in conversations about race, simply because he was white. And because he was white, the world said Hunter must shut up and listen to Darius when it came to race. But honestly, Hunter wasn't sure why.

He understood that a listening posture was standard biblical wisdom and humility—to be slow to speak like the wise man in Proverbs, not the fool. And sure, that was reason enough. But didn't this same scriptural obligation also apply to Darius? Didn't Darius have as much responsibility as he did to be quick to listen? Wasn't the goal for him and Darius to be equals? It shouldn't matter who speaks first, right? Especially because this was Darius! His old friend. One of his groomsmen. His running buddy. In fact, Darius had insisted the two of them run together, health nut that he was. And if this wasn't enough, the two of them had served as deacons together for years at their church. Of all people, they should be able to let their hair down and talk. All Hunter wanted was a simple one-on-one conversation with his friend, so he could hear—and help—him out.

But Hunter struggled even to ask for this much because he felt like there was a double standard: he wasn't allowed to say anything about race, but Darius was seemingly allowed to say everything. Hunter was thirty-nine years old and had been told throughout his life that racism was his fault. The media's tone toward him was harsh and accusatory, and Hunter didn't get it. What he did get was defensive. That's what had happened when Hunter and Darius had tried to talk about JaVari Dupree. Hunter knew that getting super defensive wasn't helpful. But he just hadn't felt like the conversation was fair. He hadn't segregated schools, after all. He'd never burned a cross.

What's more, Hunter had racist things said to him in his past, not that anybody cared. Even worse, when he was in college, his friend—who was white—was shot to death at work by a fifteen-year-old kid who was black. Hunter had grown up with this friend, and he missed his friend. And while Hunter obviously wasn't happy about Brewers's death, he couldn't figure out why he was supposed to be more upset about a man being killed a few states away just because the races were reversed.

Hunter would be the first one to make clear that he cared about black people. He even felt like he had an insight or two about black communities that might genuinely help them. But sharing them would require doing what he felt everyone was saying he must not do—speak. He knew that if he transgressed this unwritten law, everything he said would be used against him. If he transgressed this law, he'd be called a racist. And yet the culture had the nerve to condemn him for being silent about racial matters.

But it should be safe to have this conversation with his wife—right? Hunter was about to turn to her and spill half of his thoughts when he noticed the clock.

"Crap," Hunter whispered to himself through a sigh. They were cutting it close to make it to the prayer meeting on time. With a head full of thoughts and a heart full of troubles, Hunter faced his wife and opened his mouth. Only a sentence came out. "Honestly, Jules, the conversation is just tough."

From then on, all Hunter heard was the clock ticking. He never thought it looked good when a deacon was late to church. He stomped back over to the bottom of the stairs. "CLAYTON CAULKINS, GET DOWN HERE RIGHT NOW!" Hunter yelled with a tone that let Clay know there would be fire and brimstone if he delayed another second. Clay, appearing almost instantly, ran down the stairs.

Everyone shuffled into the car. Hunter was about to pull out of the driveway when Julie shouted, "Shoot!"

"What?" Hunter asked as he slammed on the brakes. "What

now? What could possibly be happening now?" he said, no longer able to mask his irritation. Julie confessed that she'd forgotten to turn off the TV. Clay was still catching his breath from bounding downstairs, but Hunter told him to run inside and turn off the TV anyway. Clay obeyed, quickly this time, and bolted back into the house. As he did, Hunter sighed. He thought of Darius. He pulled out his phone and shot him a text.

> Hey bro. Running late but hope to see you this morning. Thinking of you with the Brewers stuff. Praying too. Would love to catch up soon. Let's look to Jesus today.

Inside the house, Clay grabbed the TV remote. The cable news station was indeed still on and running. Some lady Clay didn't know was talking. Or arguing. Or yelling. Clay didn't know how to describe her tone, but he did know it sounded angry.

WE JUST HAVE TO BE HONEST THAT HAD MALACHI BREWERS FOLLOWED THE LAW, HE WOULD STILL BE ALIVE. PEOPLE GET SO UPSET, BUT I'M JUST GOING TO SAY IT: HE WAS A CRIMINAL! HE HAD BEEN ARRESTED A NUMBER OF TIMES BEFORE. HE HAD A LONG RECORD THAT INCLUDES . . .

Clay heard the horn blaring.

"Let's go, Clay!" Hunter shouted, certain Jesus would return before he ever made it to church.

"Coming!" Clay instinctively replied as he clicked off the TV.

Clay sprinted back into the car. Hunter drove the family to church, speeding most of the way. He knew he should drive safer, especially in front of his kids, but he thought the risk of modeling bad driving was worth the benefit of getting to church sooner. The drive from their home to the church was a long haul, and Hunter did want to hear what their pastor would say, if anything, about this last week. Julie often fussed at Hunter for his lead foot. He had yet to tell her about the ticket he had talked his way out of last week.

So, Hunter floored it. All the while, Clay sat quietly in the back, catching his breath, assuming Malachi Brewers had deserved to die.

Questions for Reflection and Discussion

1. Read 2 Chronicles 20. When we're overwhelmed, to whom should we turn? Take a moment to turn to God in prayer as you think about the matters this chapter has raised.
2. At what points, if any, did you resonate with Hunter's story?
3. What does Hunter get right? What does he get wrong?
4. Describe the mask Hunter is wearing and who he's hiding from. (Hint: he's hiding from more than one person.)
5. Is Hunter's fear of being called a racist right or wrong? Why?
6. How would you help Hunter think through the conversation he wants to have with Darius? Does it matter if Darius speaks first in that conversation? Why or why not? Which Scripture passages inform your answer?
7. What parts of this chapter, if any, challenged or bothered you?
8. Do you pray for people like Hunter in your life? Why or why not? If you do pray for them, what do you pray?

ENCOURAGEMENT
FOR HUNTER

*Finally, all of you, have unity of mind, sympathy,
brotherly love, a tender heart, and a humble mind.*

—1 PETER 3:8

*When your friend has just fallen and broken her
arm, it is time to comfort her and get her care, not to
offer a lecture on the dangers of skateboarding. That
should come later, and perhaps shouldn't come from
you at all (depending on what your relationship is).*

—ALAN JACOBS[1]

Our first counseling session begins with Hunter, a white brother who is sincerely trying to wrap his mind around matters of race. He wants to say the right thing to his wife, Julie. He wants to say the right thing to his friend Darius. And this desire is good and godly. The Christian's speech should always edify (Ephesians 4:29). And yet notice that Hunter seems to be consumed with what he could *say* as opposed to what he could *hear.* What if Hunter's first step was to listen? That is where I'd begin in counseling Hunter—with his ears.

Listen First

Hunter and Darius both love the Lord. Both hate racism. Both want good for the other. Both have the same level of education. Hunter is white. Darius is black. Malachi Brewers's case has given them a racial issue to talk about, and Hunter is struggling with what he perceives as a communication imbalance.

Hunter feels like society is telling him to listen to Darius on matters of race, but he's not sure why. He gets that a listening posture is standard biblical wisdom and humility (Proverbs 18:12–13; James 1:19), and sure, that is reason enough. But don't these scriptural commands and postures also apply to Darius? Hunter struggles because he feels like there is a double standard: he's not allowed to say anything, but Darius is seemingly allowed to say everything. Hunter is intellectually bright. He has had racist things said to him in his past. He has an insight or two about black communities that might genuinely help them. What's more, this is just a one-on-one conversation with his good friend Darius! Isn't the goal for them to be equals? It shouldn't matter who speaks first, right?

Underlying Hunter's struggle is the concept of tone. The importance of finding the right tone in conversations about race is vastly underappreciated. Yet if we don't find the right tone, racial damage results.

We've all seen it. Better yet, we've all *heard* it. Someone sincerely means to impart a helpful comment on a racial matter, yet unwittingly they do more damage than good. They say one thing, but the listener hears quite another. It happens when a white brother or sister says, "I don't see color!" or criticizes some aspect of black life or culture—whether an institution (like the black church or black families) or certain communities or its members (neighborhoods, theologians, historical figures, everyday teenagers, women, and men). Am I saying these institutions and people are above critique?

Not at all. But I am trying to help white brothers and sisters better understand why they should be slower to critique them.

My white brother and sister, whom I love, you can easily say more than you mean to say on race and, in doing so, grieve your neighbor rather than love them.

And I fear Hunter will grieve Darius if he doesn't begin to understand that their conversation isn't simply between the two of them; it's between them and their personal histories, experiences, and communities, which in no small part shape who they are. Could it be that Hunter, like many white brothers and sisters, sees some important aspects of life individualistically?[2] This individualistic perspective isn't always bad. But it means Hunter likely misses the larger context that is present and informing his conversation with Darius. You see, Hunter simply feels like the narrative being written is that Darius should speak first because white people are dumb, foaming-at-the-mouth racists. Well, that's not true, and such a statement *should* anger someone. Indeed, many white people are angry and defensive in conversations about race because they feel this is how they're perceived and represented. And yet Darius doesn't see Hunter that way at all.

Why then should Darius, and people like him, generally speak first on matters of race? They should speak first not because they know everything (spoiler alert: they don't) but because *black voices have been marginalized for so long.*

Hunter would be helped to understand there is asymmetry, historically (not inherently), between whites and blacks. Otherwise, he'll continue scratching his head, wondering things like, *Why do we have Black History Month?* Yet could it be that we have Black History Month because in many school textbooks and curricula, the other eleven months are more centered on the history of whites? Could it be that what's white has often been assumed, unspoken, and standardized as what's normal? Hence, historical asymmetry.

Weigh History

If Hunter doesn't realize that, when it comes to race, the weight of history can land differently on Darius than it does on him, he's going to struggle to love Darius well when it comes to talking about race. You'll remember that Hunter has had racist things said to him. And this is horrible! Racism is *never* okay. Hunter and Darius equally bear God's image, and so we rightly lament what has happened to Hunter.

Yet we also understand that racism against Hunter likely does not carry the same weight as the racism Darius has experienced. If Darius is called a nigger, it's different than Hunter being called a cracker. History compounds the insult to Darius but not as much to Hunter. Injustice compounds the insult to Darius but not as much to Hunter. Masses of people have been lynched, mobbed, and discriminated against for being niggers, not for being crackers.

You understand this principle. It's why we focus more care and attention on men abusing women than women abusing men. It's not that a woman hitting a man is better than the opposite, but that the opposite is far more prevalent, and the opposite reflects an abuse of power dynamics. Power abuses are especially heinous because the perpetrators use authority and strength to serve themselves rather than to bless others.

So, as we seek to love one another across racial lines, it is useful to remember that there is such a thing as asymmetry in history. If we don't remember this, I fear that many white brothers and sisters will continue to engage in ideological debates and polemics on race as conversations that are largely intellectual, individual exercises, free from the freight of history.

If white brothers and sisters are to put their neighbors' needs before their own, they should keep the listener in mind (Philippians 2:3–4). Ephesians 4:29 says Christians are to speak as fits the occasion (context matters) so that what we say may give grace to those who hear (audience matters as well). Tone-deafness happens when a speaker does not give the proper weight to, or ignores altogether, important factors about their audience and, in so doing, says something they don't mean to say.

For instance, white brothers and sisters may not mean to defend racism, but when they instantly critique Martin Luther King Jr., they seem not to be aware that they sound more concerned about King than they do the racism he opposed and that ultimately took his life. Someone like Hunter might feel this difficulty in critiquing King is unfair. Yet if Hunter wants to blame someone for what he perceives as injustice, he shouldn't blame Darius; he should blame those who embedded the racial caste deep in America's structure and psyche from its early days.

The strife and difficulties we experience today are in no small part the bitter harvest of past racist seeds sown. The division of our forefathers has its effects on us, their children. Even though we did not participate directly in acts of the past, we are in no way freed from living in their shadow. My white brothers and sisters should take care—and I praise God for the many who do—to see whether their critiques sound like, or are at least downstream from, racists of the past (whom I trust they have no intent or desire to emulate!). To put it differently, none of us are our own independent, self-sustaining streams; we all are connected to the tides of the past, and these tides will wash up on the shores of our lives, communities, and hearts—whether we like it or not.

Prioritize Love and Mercy over Judgment

Remember when Hunter's son Clay overheard the pundit? Here were her words:

WE JUST HAVE TO BE HONEST THAT HAD
MALACHI BREWERS FOLLOWED THE LAW,

HE WOULD STILL BE ALIVE. PEOPLE GET SO
UPSET, BUT I'M JUST GOING TO SAY IT: HE
WAS A CRIMINAL! HE HAD BEEN ARRESTED
A NUMBER OF TIMES BEFORE. HE HAD A
LONG RECORD THAT INCLUDES . . .

I highlight these words not because a fictional news pundit said them, but because those who profess the name of Christ have said things like this in the wake of high-profile shootings of African Americans. And the question I want to ask is, should *Christians*—who understand themselves most fundamentally to be lawbreakers *saved by* grace—say such things?[3] We know what it is for mercy to triumph over judgment, don't we? That's not to say that Christians think crimes shouldn't be punished. Christians rightly believe in the God-ordained reality of individual agency and personal responsibility. We believe that what we do matters and has consequences. Moreover, we believe God has ordained governments. If we break the law, we may very well receive punishment, for authorities do "not bear the sword in vain" (Romans 13:4). But we also believe that punishments should be *just*, and that in a fallen world they can at times be unjust. And that is the question: not whether Brewers was punished, but whether his punishment was just. Did the punishment fit the crime? This, of course, assumes Brewers did commit a crime, which leads to another point.

You'll remember the pundit cited Brewers's criminal background and seemed to do so as justification for his death. But to invoke Brewers's background in this way is problematic for two reasons. First, citing his background in this way presumes guilt. Yet just because someone has done something wrong in the past does not necessarily mean they have done wrong in the present. Christians, of all people, should believe that people can change! And so we give the benefit of the doubt, and treat people as innocent until proven guilty. It's prejudice that would have us do otherwise.

Second, invoking Brewers's criminal background as justification for his death reduces him to nothing but a criminal. Yet having a criminal background does not mean Brewers deserved to die as he did, for Brewers was not merely a criminal. He was, more fundamentally, a *person*—one made in God's image and therefore worthy of respect, dignity, and justice—regardless of his past.

I'll push one step further as we're considering personal agency in light of these matters. Let's say a common pitfall of theologically conservative Christians is to see aspects of life in individualistic terms. Hence, we may say things like, "Criminals in the inner city act like animals!" While I don't endorse that dehumanizing language in racial conversations, for the sake of argument, can I ask, could part of the reason they act like animals be because they've been put in a cage? That is, could systemic challenges they're suffering from be part of the reason they are acting as they do? I'm not saying it's the only reason. Again, people are responsible for their actions. But it seems to me that evangelicals can often see "animal behavior" but not the cages that may be a factor in causing it.

Scripture, I think, sees both. In Exodus 6:9, for instance, we see God's people reject Moses "because of their broken spirit *and* harsh slavery" (emphasis mine). It's easy to see animal behavior, fault someone for it, and move on. It's harder to see the cage. Yet people's conditions are factors to appreciate when considering their behavior. What if we ourselves had been in the scenario of the person we might look down on? Commenting on the sordid conditions of black boys and girls in "the cage"—conditions that arose from segregation—James Baldwin powerfully described how someone's surroundings can corrode their will, their hope:

> It is not to be wondered at, therefore, that the violent distractions of puberty, occurring in such a cage, annually take their toll, sending female children into the maternity wards and male children into the streets. It is not to be wondered at that a boy,

one day, decides that if all this studying is going to prepare him only to be a porter or an elevator boy—or his teacher—well, then [forget about it]. And there they go, with an overwhelming bitterness which they will dissemble all their lives, an unceasing effort which completes their ruin. They become the menial or the criminal or the shiftless, the Negroes whom segregation has produced and whom the South uses to prove that segregation is right.[4]

Embrace a Humble Tone

I implore the Hunters out there to remember that matters of race, racism, and identity aren't simply abstract, theological tenets. If you treat them as such, you might hurt friends like Darius more than they're already hurting, compounding their pain. After all, too many black brothers and sisters have been let down by churches that preach hard against every sin except racism and its effects.

Could it be, my white brother or sister, that you're not the best person to offer that critique of the black community, and that God can use someone else whom the black community might more naturally trust to better speak to their issues? I'm not saying you should never speak on them. There are, of course, exceptions to the general principles I've laid out here.[5] That's why they're wisdom and not law. Lest we gut the church's missionary charge altogether, we don't want to say that one must share someone else's background in order to speak truth.

That said, tone is widely undervalued today, and tone-deafness is widely spread. Why? Because too many evangelicals do not give proper weight to our listener's background and experiences. We act as if all that matters is that we speak the truth. But the apostle Paul's logic in 1 Corinthians 13:1–7 should slow us in our speech. After all, if we have all truth but not the love in which we are to speak it, we are nothing.

Conclusion: Lead with Lament

How can the Hunters of the world embrace a humble tone and so improve their conversations about race? They can enter conversations with a posture of lament. We'll revisit this concept of lament often in this book, but for now, suffice it to say that if you're like Hunter and you're planning to talk with someone like Darius, lead with lament. Enter the conversation recognizing something of the sorrowful weight of these conversations. I'm not saying you need to apologize for things you didn't do or assume every black person has the same mind on the racial complexities of the day. (As we'll see, black people are quite diverse in their opinions!) But I am saying you should recognize your racial experience probably isn't the same as your listener's. And I am saying that if you appreciate the weight your listener may feel in these conversations (especially after a racial tragedy), you may have a much better conversation. If you lead with an accusatory or skeptical posture, your listener will likely perceive you to be an adversary. If you lead with a posture of lament, they'll likely lower their mask and, perhaps, speak.

Friend, isn't this lamenting posture what we see our Lord Jesus Christ model? Though he knew he would raise Lazarus, he still took time to enter the pain of Mary. He didn't say, "What's your problem? Don't you know I'm about to raise him from the dead?" No, he *listened* to her grief. He wept (John 11:35). What if you did the same?

Questions for Reflection and Discussion

1. Has there been a time when you spoke about race in a tone-deaf way, or someone spoke in a tone-deaf way to you? What was the result?

2. How can keeping in mind our own background and someone else's background affect how we think about race?

3. In conversations about race, is your bent to speak about individual actions (animal behavior) or structures (the cage) first? Why? How might keeping both these realities in mind change how you speak about race?

4. When should you lead with lament in conversations about race? What would it look like for you to do so?

5. Would you have counseled Hunter differently than I? Why? In what ways? From which passages of Scripture?

CHAPTER 3

A MINORITY MASK— MEET DARIUS

I am weary.

—PSALM 6:6

When [as a black person] you have to navigate this presumption of guilt, day in and day out, and when the burden is on you to make the people around you see you as fully human and equal, you get exhausted. You are tired.

—BRYAN STEVENSON[1]

Sure enough, Darius Lowry's phone buzzed. He figured his pastor would text him sooner or later to ask him where he was. The prayer meeting to lament Malachi Brewers's death was scheduled to start in just a few minutes.

Darius usually came to church early, and today was no different. He pulled into the church parking lot with plenty of time. Rather than walking right into the building, though, Darius hung back and sat in his car. He needed space to clear his head, space to pray. He was doing his best to emotionally prepare for this Sunday. After all, this was no typical Lord's Day at Lincoln Ridge Bible Church. Darius's pastor had asked him to give a "word of hope"—a brief exhortation to the congregation, given the past week's events—at the prayer meeting. Darius and his pastor had planned to meet up a few minutes before the prayer meeting to review his hopeful word. But Darius wasn't ready to go inside. Not yet.

His mind was too busy. His heart was too heavy. And so Darius sat in the church lot, trying to do one simple thing: "*Breathe*, Darius. *Breathe*, brother," he said to himself. Breathing was hard for a brother like Darius on a Sunday like today, a Sunday following another black man being slain. Since breathing was so much work, Darius instead opted to anxiously run over his notes for his short address. Honestly, though, he knew he didn't really want to give it.

But he felt he should.

Darius was one of a dwindling number of black people in the church. He sensed some responsibility to field requests like those of his pastor. After all, he was a deacon. Such a burden came with being a black leader in a white church. Or did it come simply with being black in a white church? Darius didn't know, but he didn't have time to think about all that. He needed to get inside. He had his boy, his prince—Jackson—in the car, who was some wonderful mix of oblivious and patient. Jackson knew what his dad was about to do, but he didn't really *know* what all it entailed. It didn't matter. Jackson had a tablet to keep him busy while his dad was busy praying. Or worrying. Or worrying out loud. Either way, Darius picked up his phone, ready to see a gentle but urgent request from his pastor about his ETA. But Darius's eyebrows raised when he checked his new text message. There was nothing from his pastor. There was everything from Hunter.

"Ah, Hunt," Darius said under his breath, as he read Hunter's text. It was the seventeenth of its kind he had received in six days. By now such notes were standard form during racial tragedies.

News would break. White brothers and sisters would ask Darius how he's doing with it all. And Darius would sigh.

It wasn't that he didn't appreciate them trying to love him.

It wasn't that he wasn't grateful they wanted to learn.

It was that he was tired.

Tired of having to try and express the inexpressible over and over. Tired of having to help people, who reached out to him, find the words to say. Tired of being everyone's one black friend, consultant, and comforter. Tired of feeling as if it was on him to persuade his white brothers and sisters to care about one of the most complicated and charged issues in the country—racism. Darius was tired of white Christians being anywhere from apathetic to antagonistic in response to these issues. White people's ignorance was a boulder, and Darius had been pushing it up the mountain of their indifference for years now, with little help. And so Darius was exhausted. Exhausted from being made to feel like a spokesperson for his entire race. Exhausted from endless "conversations" that seemingly bore no fruit. Exhausted by watching people like Hunter enter and leave discussions about racial matters as easily as they would chats about sports or abstract theological doctrines.

Darius was weary of it all, and so were some of his black and Hispanic friends. Despite Darius's best efforts to convince them otherwise, not a few of them were thinking about leaving the very church he had just pulled into that morning—the one which he sat outside of, alone and tired. Those two descriptors marked too much of Darius's existence, not just in a white church but in a white world.

As the isolation nagged him, a painful memory resurfaced in Darius's mind. Last summer, when JaVari Dupree was murdered, Hunter had asked to talk to Darius. Reluctantly, Darius had agreed. This was Hunter, after all. Their conversation started well. Hunter was inquisitive. Hunter had been eager. He'd told Darius everything he'd wanted to know.

"I want to know what it's like to be black. I want to know how to fix this problem of racism. I want to know—"

"Man, have you ever considered this conversation ain't about what you want," Darius had said, interrupting his running buddy.

"Okay," Hunter had said, surprised and a little hurt. *"Brother, I mean, I feel like—and I'm just being honest—you always talk about race, so I figured it wouldn't hurt to—"*

"Yeah, well maybe I would talk about it less if you and your little crew of white supremacist deacons talked about it more. But that would require something that's never going to happen: y'all to change."

Their conversation had ended soon after this exchange.

Darius had wanted to say more to his friend, yet he feared being frank with him. Darius felt like Hunter could speak freely about race. But if Darius said anything, he had to say it perfectly—that is, he had to speak on Hunter's terms. Otherwise Hunter would get defensive. Otherwise Hunter wouldn't be able to digest what he was saying. Otherwise Hunter and people like him, white people, would find one fault with his words and dismiss his entire point. Having danced this dance before, Darius knew he'd better add the perfect disclaimers to what he said, lest he be labeled divisive in the church. This label often felt like a baptized way of calling someone a race-baiter. Such knowledge only compounded what he felt Monday through Saturday: that to get by, he'd better operate by the norms white people were used to—or else.

White people. Darius's son, Jackson, loved them. Darius knew so because Jackson told him so. And honestly, this made Darius happy. He knew God wanted people to love each other. And Jackson told his dad how white people had shown him love as much as any other person. But Darius was torn. He had grown up in an all-black neighborhood and had attended all-black schools and an

HBCU. But by age fourteen, Darius had learned he had to turn on a certain bravado so he could seem like a man. That way dudes in his hood wouldn't mess with him. Yet it was that same bravado Darius had to turn off when the police messed with him. That way he wouldn't get killed.

On.

Off.

From fourteen years old. The last age Emmett Till lived to see. How would he teach his Emmett—Jackson—to survive in this sin-sickened world? He didn't want to rob Jackson of his affection and innocence toward his white peers. But how would he teach him to be as innocent as a dove yet as wise as a serpent? How would he teach his son to simultaneously be both a boy and a man? And Darius had to teach his white friends about race on top of all this? He was tired of it all.

To top it all off, some of Darius's friends—the ones leaving the church for others—thought he was crazy for staying in his church, which made Darius struggle that much more. For the sake of church unity, he had pleaded with them to stay. Yet there he sat, exhausted and alone—too black for his white friends, not black enough for his black ones.

Mask on.

Mask off.

This was Darius's life as a boy. It was still his life as a man.

A knock on Darius's window startled him. Darius looked up, expecting to see his pastor, concerned and anxious.

George Mack, a member of LRBC, stood on the other side of the glass instead.

Middle-aged. White. Southern. "Brother Mack," as George was called, asked if Darius could step out of his car to talk. Darius respectfully obliged and got out of his vehicle. Jackson hung back, sitting inside the car, consumed by his tablet. Hunter had just screeched into the parking lot. His family fell out of the van, disheveled as always, but they had made it to church just in time for the prayer meeting. Unloading his family, Hunter saw Darius standing with Brother Mack. Hunter figured it would be good to touch base about his text message to Darius before they went inside. Hunter would send his wife in to find seats for their family.

"Clay can hang with me," Hunter said to Julie, and off she went with their daughters. Hunter and Clay stood respectfully behind Brother Mack, as it was clear he was talking to Darius, though they stood within earshot. Jackson looked up from his tablet, saw his buddy, and ran out of the car to greet his best friend. Hunter, on the other hand, couldn't help but overhear Brother Mack talking to Darius.

"Darius, my spirit is troubled," Brother Mack said.

"What's wrong, Brother Mack?" Darius asked with his typical pastoral warmth, despite the fact he had about as much emotion as the desert had rain. Darius didn't know Brother Mack all that well, but he assumed Brother Mack was about to express his sympathies about Malachi Brewers.

"Well, your wife is pregnant, right?" Brother Mack asked.

Slightly surprised, Darius nodded with a smile. "That's right. Eight months today," he said with a father's pride. "She's at home today, unfortunately, not feeling well with the baby and all."

"Okay, well, Darius, I've been mad at you for like three weeks," Brother Mack said, catching Darius totally off guard. Brother Mack continued.

"You see, I'm the one who volunteers to put soda in the vending machines downstairs. And a few weeks ago, I saw a black guy with a pregnant wife down there. They got some sodas but spilled them everywhere. I called after them, but they totally blew me off, and I was left to clean up the mess. I didn't get a good look at who it was, but I figured it was you because—I mean, how many black guys have pregnant wives in the church?"

Darius was shocked. He never went near those machines. He wasn't sure what was worse: Brother Mack's audacity, insensitivity, or racial profiling.

"Brother Mack, I uh," Darius stuttered. "I—I don't drink soda," he said, scratching his head.

"Oh," Brother Mack said, looking slightly stunned and a tad embarrassed. Apparently he'd been sure his case was airtight. "Er—well, okay, I guess it may not have been you after all. But at least it felt good to get that off my chest."

Brother Mack stopped speaking, and Darius couldn't start speaking.

"Well, I should go find my daughters," Brother Mack said, breaking the silence. "See you inside, Darius." Brother Mack went inside the church, seemingly without a second thought.

Darius stood, dazed. Confused. Breathless. He had heard no word from his pastor yet, but Hunter had heard the entire exchange between Mr. Mack and Darius.

And Hunter had said nothing.

Darius's eyes welled up as he stood ashamed and emasculated in front of his friend. In view of his son. How could Darius give a word of hope this morning when he had to continue into the sanctuary—devastated?

Questions for Reflection and Discussion

1. Read Psalm 6. What does the psalmist's confession teach us about what we can do with our sorrows?
2. At what points, if any, did Darius's story resonate with you?
3. What does Darius get right? What does he get wrong?
4. Describe the mask Darius is wearing and who he is hiding from. (Hint: he's hiding from more than one person.)
5. When it comes to being honest about race, is "getting things off our chest" a loving thing to do? Why or why not? Which passages of Scripture inform your answer?
6. Should Darius's pastor have asked Darius to give a word of hope? Why or why not?
7. Are Darius's white brothers and sisters wrong for reaching out to him during the racial tragedy? Is there a better way they could reach out? Which passages of Scripture inform your answer?
8. Should Darius follow some of his friends to a different church? Why or why not? Is he wrong to convince those leaving to try to stay? Why or why not? Which passages of Scripture inform your answer?
9. Do you pray for people like Darius in your life? Why or why not? If you do pray for them, what do you pray?

ENCOURAGEMENT FOR DARIUS

Walk . . . with all humility and gentleness, with patience, bearing with one another in love, eager to maintain the unity of the Spirit in the bond of peace.

—EPHESIANS 4:1–3

Just because what I'm saying is honest, doesn't mean it's fruitful.

—JACKIE HILL PERRY[1]

If it's not obvious, Darius's story hits close to home for me. So I'm not sure if this next section is as much counseling as it is catharsis, but either way, I hope it'd be helpful for Darius, and I hope it's helpful for you. Let's begin. I'd encourage Darius with the following six truths.

1. "You're Not Crazy"

That's what I'd tell him. You're. Not. Crazy. In fact, you're quite sane. The frustration Darius feels and the cultural differences he perceives—which are obvious to him but invisible to his white brethren—are legitimate. First Corinthians 10:13 says, "No temptation has overtaken you that is not common to man." In other words, the trials Darius faces have been and are suffered by others. Darius isn't alone in what he's going through.

All people, of any ethnicity, have been misunderstood by others at their churches. More specifically to Darius's trial, however, many ethnic minorities in predominantly white churches feel what he's felt. Many have propped up their masks, and this is a tragedy. A church should be the safest place to share and bear burdens. Yet when it comes to race, for too many minorities in predominantly white churches—it is the opposite. The place where brothers and sisters should receive the most comfort for their racial hurt—their church—has been the place where they've incurred the most pain. Hence, many minority brethren would rather wear a mask than expose themselves to further injury. And so the gathering that should be mask-free has become a masquerade ball. And Darius can't breathe well through that mask; he's tired of trying to hold it up, and that's what I'd tell Darius next.

2. "You're Not Crazy, but You Are Tired"

And how could he not be, especially in the days of Malachi Brewers? Darius's grief was never *just* about Malachi Brewers. It was about JaVari Dupree. It was about Walter Scott. It was about Eric Garner. It was about Rodney King. It was about Emmett Till. And we could keep going.

Let's say, in light of all this grief, Darius has been running at his church with the football of a different racial perspective, and he's been getting tackled by majority members from his church because he hasn't gotten much blocking. Few members of the majority have spoken up for the minorities, stepping in to take the hit for them. As one who *has* received this blocking in his own experience, I can tell you that *this blocking makes all the difference*. But no one can run the length of the field and not be out of breath at the end.

We're human, and so we tire; our frames are but dust. God remembers that, Psalm 103:14 says. But we don't always remember that—and in our amnesia, we can expect or demand things of ourselves that we shouldn't. Not a few minorities feel undue guilt for getting tired or angry in the work of maintaining racial unity.

People often ask me how I, as an African American, stay in a predominantly white church without getting mad at the typical racial challenges that arise in doing so. My short answer is, I don't. But I also don't assume that my anger is always righteous anger or will always remain righteous anger. I have to check myself. I try to weigh four factors when it comes to the question, "How can you stay in white churches as a black man?"

Factor 1: I grew up in these spaces. I've been in predominantly white churches most of my life, and praise God, they have been good to me and my family. I recognize that's not the case for all black people, but I'm noting this point because it shows how we all have different bandwidths, given the life circumstances God has sovereignly ordained for us. Some of us will be able to take more, some less, and that's okay.

Factor 2: I trust the leadership. This is crucial. If you can't generally trust the leadership of your church, you should leave (even if your reasons for not trusting them are wrong). To be sure, before you go, you should make sure you've done all you can to try to build trust. That means doing things like having forthright conversations (per Matthew 5:23–24 and 18:15), hoping for the best (1 Corinthians 13:7), and praying (1 Thessalonians 5:17). But if after doing so you still don't trust the leadership, or especially if you believe them to be in unrepentant sin, leave for another sound church. In my experience, however, I've been able to trust the predominantly white leadership of churches I've joined. I've been able to trust that they care about ethnic unity among Christians and want to reach all ethnicities with the gospel. I've been able to trust that they're giving serious thought and voice to matters of race and racism, and that they would be doing so even if I (or other minorities) weren't there. I've been able to trust that they're not wedded to a political ideology, persona, or cause that unnecessarily alienates minorities.

The importance of that last sentence cannot be overstated. According to 2 Corinthians 5:11–21, Christians should be ministers of reconciliation, but sadly too many Christians have become ministers of alienation. We have, whether unwittingly or wittingly, become known more for being Republicans or Democrats rather than Christians. As I'm focusing on white churches in this section, I'll speak to the temptation to conflate Christianity with political conservatism and the effect of doing so on black brothers and sisters. Put simply, for too many black people, white churches have felt more like religious outposts of the GOP than churches of Jesus Christ. Not a few black people have been made to feel that to be a part of their white church or denomination, they must subscribe to certain conservative loyalties or candidates. And this conflation of political partisanship and church membership has not only confused the message of the gospel that is free to all, but it has broken the trust of many black people who once loved the churches of which they were a part. Nonetheless, numerous black people have grown weary of the alienation, and they have, with heavy hearts, left because of it.

From what I can see, this broken trust was the lynchpin in the exodus of many black church members from white evangelical churches after the 2016 presidential election.[2] What's sad is that the steps to build trust with minorities really aren't all that difficult— many minorities just want to hear the issues of race *talked about.* Cared about. Considered. Prayed over. Applied in sermons. Yet many haven't even heard this. Instead, they've been rebuffed and dismissed for wanting to hear this, and so they have done what they feel their church, in deed though maybe not in word, wants them to do—they have exited.[3]

Factor 3: I remember my own sins. I have been helped to remember that though others in the church will sin against me, I—by definition—sin against others. Remembering my sin helps me to bear with others as I remember that they, like God, are bearing with me as well (Ephesians 4:32).

Factor 4: I remember that this is my family. One is not bound to a local church like they are bound in a marriage. Nevertheless, a church should be a family. We are members of the household of God (Ephesians 2:19), and family shouldn't easily quit on one another. That doesn't mean we can't part ways, like Abraham and Lot did. But it does mean we fight to love one another, and we're going to have to do that at *any* church we join.

To be clear, I'm not saying anyone who does decide to part ways isn't remembering their sin or isn't remembering their family. In fact, I remember speaking about these reasons once, and another black brother reproved me. He shared how for him and other black brothers and sisters he knew, black people were treated as family in name but as second cousins, if not second-class citizens, in *practice*. He stated that my very positive experience in predominantly white churches was the exception, not the norm. And you know what? I fear he was right. But I also hope he is less right with each passing day. Moreover, there are wonderful ways—beyond integration in the same church—that churches that are predominantly one ethnicity can partner with one another and demonstrate the unconquerable unity all Christians share in Christ.

At the end of the day, we are free in Christ to attend the church of our choosing. That would be my next word for Darius.

Should Racial Minorities Stay at Their White Churches?

- Does your church preach the gospel? If no, leave. If yes . . .
- Have you prayed about whether you should leave and sought counsel? If no, do that. If yes . . .

- Do you trust the leadership at your church? If no (after doing all you can to build trust), leave. If yes . . .
- Are you treated as family at your church? If no (that is, you're treated more like a second-class citizen), leave. If yes...
- Can you bear with your brothers' and sisters' shortcomings as they bear with yours? If no, leave trusting God's sovereignty and grace. If yes . . .
- Are you encouraged by your church? Do you want to stay? If on balance, no, leave enjoying your freedom in Christ. If yes or you're unsure, you have a decision to make between you and the Lord. However, it seems like, *despite it being hard, there is good reason to stay.*

Of course, there are more questions one could ask: Can my family thrive in this church? Have I seen growth in this church regarding racial issues? Am I expecting growth too quickly? If nothing were to change in this church, could I labor in it contentedly? May God give you wisdom as you seek him for the answers.

3. "You're Free, Brother"

I'd tell him, "You're free in Christ!" Darius is free to leave his church (as long as he joins another faithful one), and he is free to stay. Countless black believers have left white churches, and countless black believers have stayed in them happily. And I'd make this point—that Darius is free to leave or stay—obnoxiously clear to Darius. I'd highlight, **bold**, underline, and *italicize* it, so he would see and relish this point. Why would I go to such lengths?

I'd do so because Satan is having a field day getting sincere minority believers to turn on one another in judgment as they haggle over whether to stay or to get out of their predominantly white churches. However, what one brother or sister decides to do may not be what another brother or sister should decide to do. Yet what do we often see? The one leaving regards the one staying as an Uncle Tom; the one staying regards the one leaving as a theological liberal. What I want to ask is: Are these really the only two options, Uncle Tom or theological liberal? That sounds like the devil's deal.

Beloved, the friendly fire and the wrongful conscience binding, and the requisite shaming that follows between minority members when they choose to leave or stay in predominantly white churches must stop. The truth is that either decision requires faith. It takes faith to leave, and it takes faith to stay.[4] And if this word isn't enough for Darius, I'd encourage him to try on Scripture: "Do not speak evil against one another," James writes. "Who are you to judge your neighbor?" (James 4:11–12).

Yet here is one other thing Darius is also free from that may help him stay at his church: he is also free from the burden of saving anyone or making them repent of racial sins. In other words, people's repentance on these matters is *not* his responsibility. He does not need to carry that weight. He is not people's black Jesus. His job is to speak the truth, be gracious, and watch God work.[5] And I'd say this because if Darius believes it's his job to get people to repent, he will be incredibly (and unnecessarily) discouraged when they don't. But if he remembers that God is the one who changes people, he'll rest easier, having reoriented his hopes on God. And this hope is vital. Without it, we wither and lose steam to love those we find most difficult to love.

We saw that in Darius's story, didn't we? Do you remember that comment Darius made to Hunter, that for him and the other white deacons to be better on racial matters, they'd have to do one thing they never will do—*change*? On one level, I get what Darius was saying. We have to be realistic: some people won't change on these matters but for an act of God's grace. But that's just it! We have to remember that with God all things are possible. That doesn't mean we keep ourselves in toxic environments or harmful situations, but it also doesn't mean we lose hope in God's power and allow ourselves to grow bitter. Could it be that one reason conversations about race across color lines are so difficult is that we've lost hope in God's sanctifying power and therefore have given up on one another?

"So," I'd tell Darius, "You're free in Christ, brother." I'd tell him to choose a church and stick with it for as long as he can. People can make an idolatrously big deal out of finding the right church—just as young people do of finding the right potential spouse. We all want to find "the right fit." The truth is, however, that each option is its own mess, so pick one and decide to love it. Jesus is coming back soon. Don't search for the perfect option that can serve you. Seek to serve instead. "God will lead you to the church he wants you in, Darius," I'd tell him. "Let's move on to our next point."

4. "You're Enlisted"

Next, I'd say, "You're enlisted. Though you're free in Christ, you, too, are a man under authority. Christ is your Lord, your captain, brother." And I'd say that to make clear that Darius need not listen to where other people, whom he is not seeking for counsel, tell him he should or shouldn't go to church. Jesus is Darius's commander. He gets to say where we go, how long we stay, and so on. "In other words, Darius," I'd say, "it's not about you. It's about God, his glory, and his plans."

I think Darius would need to hear this, because as you recall, Darius felt too black for his white friends and too white for his black friends. But Darius doesn't need to put up his blackness for vote or let other people police, evaluate, or determine it. Darius was fearfully and wonderfully made by God. He need not connect his blackness to the core of his identity (despite how the world has tried to convince him to do so) nor to his church membership status. His ethnic identity is a good thing; it's just no longer *the* thing, now that he's in Christ, who is above all things in his life.[6]

Now, to be sure, Darius also needs to guard against hearing things people aren't saying. After all, no one in his story actually called him an Uncle Tom. He may have very well applied that label to himself, listening more to his insecurities than to what people were or weren't saying. And this is yet another reason why talking about race is so hard: We hear things people aren't saying, and we say things people aren't hearing. A good measure of humble self-examination and forbearance can help with both errors.

5. "You Trippin'"

This is my next word for Darius, since we're speaking about self-examination. I'd have to be honest with the brother and remind him that he's out of step if he thinks that because he's on the receiving end of racial trials, he gets to speak however he wants. The fact is that he was rude to Hunter in their conversations. Period. End of story. We might say such frustration is understandable; we might realize that worse things could have been said. But a sin is a sin is a sin. And black people can say ethnically hateful things just like white people can, just like Hispanics can, just like Koreans can, and so on. Racism is a sin anyone can commit against anyone. Whatever asymmetry exists, that's not the only thing that exists, and so we who are on the other side of tone-deaf comments from white brothers and sisters ought to take heed lest we also fall. Civil-rights leader Howard Thurman provides this same warning in his classic work, *Jesus and the Disinherited*:

> In my analyses of hatred it is customary to apply it only to the attitude of the strong towards the weak. The general impression is that many white people hate Negroes and that Negroes are merely the victims. Such

an assumption is quite ridiculous. I was once seated in a Jim Crow car which extended across the highway at a railway station in Texas. Two Negro girls of about fourteen or fifteen sat behind me. One of them looked out of the window and said, "Look at those kids." She referred to two little white girls, who were skating towards the train. "Wouldn't it be funny if they fell and spattered their brains all over the pavement!"[7]

Darius must realize that there is a real temptation for minorities to obsess over white supremacy to the point where we see racism as wholly one-sided. There's a temptation to obsess over the sins of "the other side" that causes us, often without our realizing it, to become self-righteous and narcissistic. There is a temptation to blame white people for everything, to not offer any constructive solutions, and to be unwilling to engage in critical self-reflection. If we give into this temptation, we will wrongly shame others and tear down those who don't agree with us, those who don't fit into our ideological cult. What's more, we will alienate the people whose help we could use. We're going to have a hard time getting white people to partner with us if all we talk about is how racist they are and how much they owe black people! But thanks be to God, there is a more excellent way to speak.

Given that he's not immune to racial hatred, Darius should remember Proverbs 29:11 for his conversations: "A fool gives full vent to his spirit, but a wise man quietly holds it back." To be sure, being quiet and gentle does not mean one cannot be bold; I think Martin Luther King Jr. was a quiet and gentle man, but he was as bold as a lion. Anyone who thinks gentleness and boldness are incompatible in a person needs to study further the life and ministry of Jesus.

That said, I'd remind my brother Darius that the Christian has a higher bar for his or her speech even than honesty, and that bar is edification (Romans 15:2). Not every honest thing needs to be said. Could it be that one of the reasons talking about race is so hard is because we speak out of our pain? Friends, just because we're honest, doesn't mean we're edifying; just because we're hurt, doesn't mean we're right. Perhaps no one captured this wisdom better than my grandmother, who often said, "Child, you don't have to say everything you know."

"And so," I'd tell Darius, "I think you owe Hunter an apology. You used loaded language (e.g., 'white supremacist') in a hostile way." Darius may have been exaggerating, and hyperbole isn't always bad. (In Matthew 5 Jesus told people to cut off their hand if it leads them to sin!) Yet when it comes to conversations about race; exaggeration often shuts down conversation. A point over-argued is a bad point—one that distorts, distracts, and divides.

6. "You're Forgiven"

This is my last word to Darius, and my happiest. The truth is, Darius doesn't just need to apologize to Hunter for his sin. He needs to apologize to God, and that's because all sin is against God first and foremost (Psalm 51:4).

And yet there is hope for sinners in Christ. Praise God for the beauty of 1 John 1:9: "If we confess our sins, he is faithful and just to forgive us our sins and to cleanse us from all unrighteousness."

Cleansed. Free. Enlisted. And forgiven. However tired Darius and those like him may be, however he may stumble and fall, brother Darius is going to be all right. In fact, he'll be more than all right because he does not only have God—God has him.

Conclusion: Reassure Your Listener of Your Love

Let's say Hunter takes me up on the counsel to listen to Darius first. Let's say Hunter leads with lament and asks a fumbling question.

Darius would have a choice to make at that point. He could shame Hunter, make him feel ridiculous, and practically ensure that Hunter never asks him anything again. Or Darius could welcome Hunter as Christ welcomed him. He could be tender, disarming, and recall how he too has not arrived. He could reassure Hunter of his love for him and steel their relationship that much more by doing so.

Friend, isn't this reassuring posture what we see our Lord Jesus Christ model? After Jesus was raised from the dead, an angel gave the women, who came to anoint Jesus's body, striking news and a striking command. The news was that Jesus had risen (Mark 16:6). The command was to tell the disciples *and Peter* that they would see Jesus again (v. 7). I love that Peter is specified here. He was specifically spectacular in his failure to Jesus, and so, it seems, he was in need of specific encouragement. He was in need of specific reassurance that he was indeed still one of Jesus's followers and closest friends. What if Darius lent this same kind of reassurance to Hunter after they spoke? What if you did this to the people who listen to you about race?

Questions for Reflection and Discussion

1. Do you resonate with the fatigue Darius feels? If so, how do you work through that fatigue?
2. How does our freedom in Christ affect how we think through where we'll go to church?
3. Would you have counseled Darius differently than I? Why? In what ways? From which passages of Scripture?

CHAPTER 4

A MAJORITY MASK—
MEET ANNA BETH AND
SAMANTHA LEE

Better is open rebuke than hidden love.

—PROVERBS 27:5

*The evangelical world can be a distinctly
challenging place in which to change people's attitudes
on race: Many of these churches have a long history
of resistance to racial equality. And many religious
conservatives are wary of the self-described social-justice
movements associated with the left.*

—EMMA GREEN[1]

"Seriously? Of all Sundays, you couldn't come today?" Samantha Lee asked her little sister as she plopped her purse and keys on the counter. Samantha Lee had just rushed home from Lincoln Ridge Bible Church. She had meant to stay and meet a woman who was joining her team at work, but that would have to wait until tomorrow. She needed to check on her sister.

"Yes, Lee-Lee, I seriously—no, I *especially* couldn't come today," Anna Beth spat back, making clear her resolve to boycott church that morning.

"Why? Why are you so upset? You're madder than most black people I know!" Samantha Lee exclaimed.

"Because our church has been silent about racism for so long, and—"

"How would you know? You haven't been in weeks! Have you even contacted the pastors?" Samantha Lee inserted, interrupting her sister's tirade.

"It's only been two weeks, and it doesn't matter," Anna Beth snapped, deftly adjusting her response. "No one would listen to me, anyway. I'm not on the inside at church like you. I don't know what's going on behind the scenes. The leadership was basically silent last year when JaVari Dupree was murdered. And what have we heard from the church about Malachi Brewers? Nothing. Not a word, and I don't have—"

"*You* don't have all the facts. That's what you don't have," Samantha Lee said, interrupting again. "And yet you've rendered a judgment on some case miles away over men's hearts you can't even see?"

Anna Beth couldn't believe her sister had just said that.

"You're right. *I don't have* . . . to have this conversation," Anna Beth said. Samantha Lee pleaded with her to not be like that. After all, she just wanted to talk with Anna Beth about the prayer service. She figured her sister would have loved it. That's why she was so frustrated Anna Beth had skipped it. But it was too late. Anna Beth's verdict had been passed, and Samantha Lee stood there while her little sister walked to the other side of the room.

Silently, Anna Beth sat on the couch. Instinctively she opened her phone. She started quickly scrolling on social media.

#EatingCandyWhileBlack, a hashtag showing support for

Malachi Brewers, was trending. Glancing at the most popular post, Anna Beth thought for a second.

Then she clicked Retweet.

Anna Beth Mack had worked at Lincoln Ridge Christian Academy for a year now. She wanted to teach at a school in the inner city, but her white parents wouldn't have it. Normally Anna Beth wouldn't care what they thought, but her parents were helping to pay off some of her student loans. Their one condition for Anna Beth was that she'd live anywhere but the inner city. It was too dangerous, they said. Anna Beth figured they assumed that because they simply didn't know very many—if any—black people.

Nonetheless, Anna Beth settled for working at the diverse-enough LRCA, where she taught fifth grade and loved it. She rented a room from her big sister, Samantha Lee—whom she called Sammy Lee for short and Lee-Lee for shorter. Samantha Lee owned the house and worked at a big bank on the other side of town. And Anna Beth was furious with her. Ignorant. Skeptical. Complacent. Complicit. Hyper-conservative, politically speaking. A fundamentalist only fundamental about certain things. With hands shaking as she held her phone, Anna Beth was as mad as her heart was broken.

It wasn't that Anna Beth struggled to understand Malachi Brewers's death; she knew it was the result of a deeply fallen world of injustice, of racism, of systems that were designed to oppress. It wasn't even that she struggled to hope in Christ; she believed that one day he would make all things right.

It was that Lincoln Ridge Bible Church had missed an opportunity to respond to the news of Brewers's death in any significant way. Of course there might be a prayer or a line in the church newsletter that drew no lines besides what everyone already agreed with: racism is bad. Jesus is good. Blah. Blah. Blah. Rinse. Wash. Repeat. By this point, Anna Beth knew that if her church spoke on this matter, they'd offend no one and therefore not help anyone, besides the people who wanted to hear pious trivialities.

Anna Beth was tired of the church offering vague sound bites of sympathy while making no definitive statement about racism. She was tired of LRBC being more concerned with how not to address racism than with how to address it. As far as Anna Beth was concerned, the church had not shown up and been allies, advocates, and change makers, and this wasn't her first time seeing this failure. Her church—just like her country—sadly, had been here before.

And so, with her pain compounded, Anna Beth struggled to entrust herself to a leadership who presented as non-racist instead of anti-racist, a leadership she had to seek out if she wanted to hear from them. Her church had to do better. And Anna Beth had to think about whether she wanted to belong to it.

She hadn't told anyone at the church except for Samantha Lee any of this, but if Anna Beth did, she would say it with deep love for her African American brothers and sisters. She would say it fully aware of her own privilege and therefore responsibility. She was sorry, and she was going to let everyone on social media know it.

In fact, she'd go even further. Anna Beth noticed some poster board in the corner of her living room. She had planned to take it to her classroom that week, but would redeem it for better, immediate use. She'd make a sign for her front yard, letting the neighborhood know where her household stood. She grabbed some markers and got to work.

"What are you writing?" Samantha Lee asked her, calmly and sadly.

Anna Beth ignored her. Or couldn't hear her. Or some mix of the two. Samantha Lee couldn't tell, so she just went to her and read over her shoulder. She had seen it before: #EatingCandyWhileBlack.

"Anna Beth. He. Wasn't. Eating. He was *stealing!*" Samantha Lee said sternly.

"Woah, woah, woah," Anna Beth said, finally speaking up. Her face held a smirk. "I thought we didn't have all the facts, Sis?"

"Oh, don't do that. Whatever. You are not putting that sign in my yard." Samantha Lee didn't want to be this strict of a landlord. She didn't want to bicker with her sister. In fact, Samantha Lee was already feeling insecure. Although she was older, she always felt left behind by Anna Beth, who seemed to be up on all the issues of the day. And she always felt so grieved by the way Anna Beth talked about America. Surely its citizens weren't so bad. Samantha Lee had tried to see Anna Beth's side of things before, but enough was enough. She was done. Fed up. Over it. And she wanted to make sure Anna Beth knew it. Anna Beth hadn't responded to Samantha Lee's restriction on posting the sign, so she repeated her order to make sure her rule was clear.

"Anna Beth? Hello? I'm not joking. Do not put that sign in my yard."

"Fine," Anna Beth said understandingly, as if she was ready to wave the white flag.

Samantha Lee was surprised.

"Seriously?" she asked.

"Yes, Lee-Lee." Anna Beth responded. "Seriously."

"Thank you," Samantha Lee said before turning around to walk away. She'd let the skirmish end there and give her sister and herself some time to cool off.

"Instead, I'll make a new sign with a nice definition of systemic racism," Anna Beth shouted glibly to Samantha Lee's back. "Your rich neighbors will looove that."

Samantha Lee stopped walking, but she didn't turn around. She didn't say anything. She was too sad about how nasty the conversation had gotten. A moment or two passed. Then Samantha turned around slowly and spoke a bit more calmly this time.

"I seriously don't get you, Anna Beth. Mom always taught us that color isn't important, that race doesn't matter. But it seems like race is all you talk about these days. I know you're passionate about this stuff, but this whole thing about systemic racism—do you really buy that? Like, really—you think most cops in this country harbor prejudice in their hearts?"

"Sounds like you could be one of them, Sis," Anna Beth said.

"Really? You really believe that? You must have forgotten, *Mizz Mack.*" (That was Samantha Lee's impression of what Anna Beth's students called her, though she usually reserved it for happier occasions when both sisters would smile.) "Have you forgotten that my bank donated the money for your classroom's supplies this year at *my* initiative? Why? Because I feel so bad for the poor little black kids like you do while I sit holier-than-thou on my phone? No. But because I don't see color; I see them as what they are—human beings made in God's image. And so I actually did something because I actually make money, *unlike yourself.* Why don't you tweet that the next time you decide to bail on church!"

Anna Beth sat with her mouth open. "Seriously, Lee-Lee? You went there?" Anna Beth said, tears now streaming down her face. She turned around, stormed upstairs, and slammed her door.

Anna Beth was unsurprised by Samantha Lee's point about money. She knew her sister believed the social problems of the day were primarily one of class, not race. That was no small part of what motivated Samantha Lee to go into banking, and she had done some really impressive work for their community. Samantha Lee had always been the impressive one. But what left the impression on Anna Beth that day wasn't her sister's viewpoint; it was her meanness. And this after she had just come home from church, confirming to Anna Beth that LRBC wasn't doing folks like her sister any good. It was a social club, not a place of love for the weak and marginalized.

An hour passed. Anna Beth spent all of it in her room, sitting on her bed, looking out her window, thinking about TaNeesha Hayes, her college roommate from her freshman year, her best friend.

TaNeesha and Anna Beth were as different as different could be. Anna Beth was, on the surface, the preppy, peppy Southern white gal (despite her family's financial struggles at the time, which no one knew about); TaNeesha was black, introverted, and from the inner city. Walking into their room that first day of freshman orientation, both young women wondered how they might get along at first, but by the end of spring break, the two of them were inseparable. That spring break Anna Beth's natural group of friends, her sorority sisters, all went to the Caribbean, but Anna Beth couldn't afford it. When TaNeesha saw how devastated Anna Beth was about not being able to go on her trip, she invited Anna Beth to go home with her for break. Anna Beth had some misgivings but knew she wanted to do something, so she went. And she was surprised.

On that trip, Anna Beth saw TaNeesha's community. She ate TaNeesha's food. She worshiped with TaNeesha's church. For the first time in Anna Beth's life, she was in a situation where she was the minority. And from that new purview, Anna Beth began realizing some things. Unlike what Anna Beth had assumed, TaNeesha's all-black church faithfully preached the gospel. Unlike what she had grown up believing, TaNeesha's family was poor, yes, but they were hardworking too. Anna Beth began to realize that despite what she had always believed, there was no such thing as *the* black community. There were multiple black communities. They were diverse. And they were beautiful.

Beautiful, like TaNeesha's brother, Aaron. She had seen pictures of him and thought he was cute, but she had never seen him in person. When he arrived home that day, he was wearing a new do-rag he had just purchased. Trying to mess with his sister's new white friend, he—with a tinge of cockiness—asked Anna Beth how he looked in his new grooming appliance.

"Scary," she immediately said.

Anna Beth felt so dumb for saying that. Why was *that* the word she chose? *Scary?* Why scary? What did she mean by that? That's what TaNeesha graciously asked her in private later on that week. Anna Beth didn't know the answer. She had never thought of herself as afraid of black guys in do-rags. Nevertheless, she fumbled through an answer or three. TaNeesha, and Aaron for that matter, did what they had seemingly done all week—they listened to her. They dealt kindly with her. They were vulnerable with her. They were everything many Christians on Twitter were not, and Anna Beth was taken with it all, won by it all. Anna Beth and Aaron would have struck up a relationship, but Anna Beth assumed her father would have opposed it. Yet Anna Beth would never forget how gently Aaron treated her. She had many good memories from that surprising spring break.

Anna Beth recalled another one. She remembered another night on that trip when Charles, TaNeesha and Aaron's father, spoke about the elementary school he had attended as a child in Memphis. Given how she had put her foot in her mouth with Aaron, Anna Beth was happy to sit back and simply listen to Mr. Hayes. And anyone could do that if Charles Hayes was speaking. His voice was velvet—a deep melody that enveloped the entire room. Charles was a large man, and that night he left a large mark on Anna Beth's life.

Charles explained how the school he attended as a boy was separate, and what became clear to Anna Beth was that it was very unequal too. With no hint of bitterness, Charles explained how he and the other colored students had inherited their textbooks from the local all-white school, as that school was getting brand-new ones. "It wasn't just that the textbooks were ratty," Charles told Anna Beth one night. "We expected that much. But some of those white kids done left the meanest notes in those books for us.

I won't repeat what they wrote. I think the 'postle Paul would say it's shameful to repeat such things. But it was racist. It was ugly."

Anna Beth couldn't believe that kids could have been treated like that, and Charles kindly answered her peppering of questions and helped her understand the effect this had on his entire generation of students. And it was this conversation that made Anna Beth want to be a teacher to kids less fortunate than her. It was this conversation that began to change her mind about race.

Anna Beth's mind was racing as she sat in her and Samantha Lee's quiet home. The house was so silent you could hear their kitchen clock tick in any one of their four bedrooms. Hearing a sound, Anna Beth jumped a little, startled. She turned away from her window, looked up, and saw Samantha Lee in her bedroom doorway.

"Anna Beth, look . . . I'm—I'm sorry," she said with sincerity. "I didn't mean what I said." Anna Beth looked up at her with hope. Samantha Lee kept talking. "I just . . . don't want to believe America is like what you say it is."

Anna Beth looked back down and shook her head. "Don't worry," she said, her tone emotionless. "I'll be gone next week. I'm moving out."

Later that night, Samantha Lee got a text from "Brother Mack"—that's how she had listed him in her contacts, since that's what everyone at church called him. She always smiled when she saw the nickname. This time was no different, and she could use a smile after the day she had just had. The text read,

> Hey! Your sister OK? Didn't see her with you at church today. She oversleep again?
> Luv ya, Dad

Why her father insisted on signing each text like a letter would never not baffle her. But as the older sister, Samantha Lee felt responsible to be Anna Beth's keeper. She wrote a simple text back to Brother Mack.

Hi, Dad. Oh no, she's woke now.

Questions for Reflection and Discussion

1. At what points did you resonate with Anna Beth's story?
2. What does Anna Beth get right? What does she get wrong? What about her sister?
3. Describe the mask Anna Beth is wearing and who she is hiding from. (Hint: she's hiding from more than one person.)
4. Are Anna Beth's parents wrong for being concerned for her safety when it came to Anna Beth teaching in an inner-city school?
5. Is Anna Beth treating her church fairly?
6. Samantha Lee defines racism primarily as a feeling in the heart. Is her definition of racism a good one? A bad one? Which passages of Scripture inform your answer?
7. Were there any other parts of this chapter that challenged or bothered you?
8. Do you pray for people like Anna Beth and Samantha Lee in your life? Why or why not?

ENCOURAGEMENT FOR ANNA BETH

He has told you, O man, what is good;
and what does the LORD require of you
but to do justice, and to love kindness,
and to walk humbly with your God?

—MICAH 6:8

We need the honesty and courage to resist the
hatred—the spirit of hatred—that the zeal even for
good causes can induce in we frail, fallen, fallible
human beings, and that corrupts the human soul and
leads inexorably to spiritual emptiness and to tyranny,
even among those who began as sincere advocates of
freedom and justice.

—ROBERT P. GEORGE AND CORNEL WEST[1]

The first thing I'm going to do if I'm counseling Anna Beth (after opening with prayer) is encourage her. That is, I'm going to highlight evidences of God's grace in her life that I see. Paul did that with the Corinthians, who were an absolute mess. Paul began his first letter to the Corinthians not by rebuking them but by thanking God for his grace to them. He reminded them of God's faithfulness and how he would keep his people (1 Corinthians 1:8–9). And if Paul could find room to encourage the Corinthians, we can certainly find room to encourage Anna Beth.

Here's one thing I would encourage her about: she means to hate racism. Praise God! May her tribe only increase! Given evangelicals' history on racial matters, let's be thankful that Anna Beth means to hate racial injustice. She doesn't want to neglect the weightier matters of the law: justice and mercy and faithfulness (Matthew 23:23). She wants to see African Americans treated rightly. This is a *good* thing, and all good things are from God (James 1:17). We should praise him for them.

But we have a few concerns to address before our counseling session is over. We'll address them by asking three questions.

1. What Can You Praise God For?

I'd ask Anna Beth how her praise and thankfulness to God have been lately. I'd ask because I would perceive, from her story, Anna Beth to be a bit proud. And if pride is one of her diseases, ingratitude is a key symptom to highlight.

A couple things tip me off to Anna Beth's pride. First, if you look back at her story, you'll notice that Anna Beth denigrates prayer. Commenting on her church's failure to respond to the tragedy of Malachi Brewers, Anna Beth implied that prayer was insignificant. Did you catch that? There is more to do than pray, but as Christians, we cannot do less. Prayer is an expression of our reliance on God, and to belittle prayer is to inflate our own sense of self-sufficiency. Is there not racial progress that LRBC has made in its history that Anna Beth can praise God for? To ignore the good that God has done is to rob him of glory.

The second thing that tips me off to Anna Beth's pride is that she seems resolved to show how righteous she is on these matters, but it's not clear how resolved she is to *help others be more righteous.*

You'll notice that Anna Beth hadn't reached out to her pastors, though she has been willing to criticize them. Anna Beth has not raised her issues with the pastors, and yet she has grown frustrated with them. It seems to me that she has wanted the pastors to fix these issues, or at least be more in tune with them, but she has not given the pastors any input on how they could do so. She has held back the straw with which they might make racially helpful bricks. Scripture is clear: if we understand someone to be in sin, we should say something *to them* first (Matthew 18:15; Galatians 6:1). Sadly, however, we often opt for saying something *about* those we disagree with instead. Yet instead of waiting on her pastors to do something, why didn't Anna Beth go and speak to them? Why didn't she invite them or the church to get involved in the work she was already doing?

We all need to be careful of the insidious and subtle self-righteousness that can creep into us as we pursue matters of righteousness and justice. Even if we're right in what we see, we can so easily forget that our being right does not make us any better than anyone else. Jesus had to die for our sins, just as much as he did for those who may not see racial matters as clearly as we do. What's more, even if we're right on these issues, we should not act as if we're always right on them. And Anna Beth should know this better than anyone!

For years Anna Beth largely thought one way about issues of race and racism—or didn't think about them at all. That changed when she got to know TaNeesha Hayes—someone who was physically and culturally different from her.[2] Notice that Anna Beth's thinking didn't change when she *met* TaNeesha, or even became *acquainted* with her. (After all, lots of us know of or about someone, but that doesn't mean we know them.) No, it was when Anna Beth got to *know* TaNeesha—on a deeper, relational level—that things began to change for Anna Beth, and she got to know TaNeesha when she went to her home for spring break.

God often uses some external factor, even a surprise spring break trip, to provoke people's minds and hearts about racial matters. That factor is particularly powerful when it is another human being, especially one we know and love. In his sovereignty, God may use something like a documentary, a book, a conversation, the prospect of adopting a child of another ethnicity, an interracial marriage, a move into a certain neighborhood, or a nationally televised injustice to educate and prick people's consciences. Brenda Salter McNeil calls the external factors that God uses to make people aware of racial matters "catalytic events."[3]

We can respond poorly or well to these catalytic events. God be praised, Anna Beth initially responded well to hers. She repented of prejudice. She sought to do what's right by others. But, as many people do when we're in the cage stage—the early days of seeing a paradigm-shifting truth—we can become the very thing we hate. This leads me to Anna Beth's relationship with her sister Samantha Lee and a second question I'd ask Anna Beth.

2. How's Your Tone?

As with the other characters, I'd prod at Anna Beth's tone. After all, Anna Beth is certain her viewpoint is 100 percent right and Samantha Lee's is 100 percent wrong. Yet I wonder if that certainty would be unsettled if Anna Beth remembered that not long ago she thought like Samantha Lee. She spoke like Samantha Lee did, even on her spring break trip. But is Anna Beth treating Samantha Lee with the grace with which TaNeesha and Aaron treated her? Is Anna Beth treating Samantha Lee with the grace with which God has treated her (Matthew 18:21–35)?

Let's assume the best. Let's assume that Anna Beth wants to help her sister grow in faithfulness regarding justice, and her way of doing so is pointing out her sister's blind spots. There is a healthy and gentle way to do pointing-out work, and there is a way to do it that is rough and proud. "If anyone is caught in any transgression, you who are spiritual should restore him in a spirit of gentleness. Keep watch on yourself, lest you too be tempted" (Galatians 6:1). Anna Beth should take care to speak to and guide others gently. Because if she refuses to help others become more righteous in a gentle way, she may very well just be flaunting her own righteousness while at the same time proving what has always been the case—that she has none. In other words, outside of Christ, Anna Beth has no righteousness. And I think that bringing up this fact would be a very freeing and useful reminder for her. That is why I'd end by asking her about her motives.

3. Who Is It All For?

Anna Beth, and folks like her, should take care that they're not pursuing racial activism to make themselves feel better. That is, they should consider whether they're pursuing racial activism more out of a sense of guilt rather than love for their neighbor. Could it be that they post on Instagram and get outraged because they fear being seen as racially ignorant? And so they strive to show that they're not. While folks like this may recognize they have not yet arrived, they at least take comfort that they are not as racist as their grandparents were. All the while, they sound like the Pharisee: "God, thank you I'm not like that sinner!" (see Luke 18:9–14).

To be sure, I'm not saying all of Anna Beth's motives are self-serving. Our motives for the good things we do are always mixed. We see many evidences of grace to highlight in Anna Beth's life, but we also see that she has room to grow in humility too. And to help her get there, I'd leave her with this warning from John McWhorter. Commenting on how we can use our racial awareness to clear our own names, he writes, "Today's consciousness-raising on race is less about helping black people than it is about white people seeking grace. . . . Fifty years ago, a white person learning about the race problem came away asking, 'How can I help?' Today the same person too often comes away asking, 'How can I show that I'm a moral person?' That isn't what the Civil Rights revolution was about; it is the product of decades of mission creep aided by the emergence of social media."[4]

I'd close my counseling session with Anna Beth by praying that both she and I would remember that justice-doers should be humble-walkers with God.

Questions for Reflection and Discussion (for Anna Beth)

1. Have you had a catalytic event in your life (or multiple events)? What was it? How did you respond?
2. Would you have counseled Anna Beth differently than I? Why? In what ways? From which passages of Scripture?

ENCOURAGEMENT FOR SAMANTHA LEE

Fools find no pleasure in understanding
but delight in airing their own opinions.

—PROVERBS 18:2 NIV

We need the honesty and courage to speak the
truth—including painful truths that unsettle not only
our foes but also our friends and, most especially,
ourselves.

—ROBERT P. GEORGE AND CORNEL WEST[1]

As we did for her little sister, we're going to begin by encouraging Samantha Lee. The evidence of God's grace in her life that I'll highlight is when she helped Anna Beth's students in a powerful way. Remember how she provided their schoolroom supplies? Whatever Samantha Lee meant by being color-blind (and we'll return to that soon), her color blindness did not keep her away from Anna Beth's students. Rather, Samantha Lee understood these students to be made in God's image—which to her meant they were worthy of love. Despite her (strong!) disagreements with Anna Beth about race, Samantha Lee was able to help those kids in a way Anna Beth couldn't. Notice that Samantha Lee and Anna Beth didn't just come together around a common goal. Rather—together—Anna Beth and Samantha Lee did more for those precious students than they could have done apart.

Samantha Lee's benevolence should challenge those of us who consider ourselves more sympathetic to racial issues. Our temptation as we read about Samantha Lee would be to assume that she is morally bankrupt, that she doesn't want to help the oppressed but instead is the oppressor. We should, however, commend Samantha Lee's aid to her fellow image bearers. I remember once being shocked when I discovered that a Samantha Lee in my own life was more involved in low-income black neighborhoods than I had been. I was not only pleasantly surprised by her love for these image bearers, but I was also humbled by how it surpassed my love for them.

But does this mean we'd have no words of correction for Samantha Lee? Far from it. Let's begin with the color blindness we were just considering.

The Issue of Color Blindness

Remember how Samantha Lee confidently affirmed color blindness by invoking what her mother had taught her? "Color isn't important . . . race doesn't matter," Samantha Lee said to Anna Beth. At this point, it's crucial to pause and consider what Samantha Lee meant by color blindness. If she basically meant "we should treat all people the same, regardless of their ethnicity or race," okay. I can agree with that. More importantly, Scripture would too. "Show no partiality," James wrote (James 2:1).

The trouble is, Samantha Lee meant more than that. She meant that we should disregard people's ethnicity or race altogether. She meant that to bring up ethnicity or race at all is problematic. And it's problematic because it perpetuates the false idea of race that has been so harmful in the past. That is, it makes race an issue when there is no issue—and therefore distracts from real issues. Moreover, wasn't color blindness Dr. King's dream? "I have a dream that my four little children will one day live in a nation where they will not be judged by the color of their skin but by the content of their character."[2] Finally, and most importantly, isn't Scripture color-blind? "There is neither Jew nor Greek, there is neither slave nor free, there is no male and female, for you are all one in Christ Jesus" (Galatians 3:28, see also Colossians 3:11). Here I'd have a few notes for Samantha Lee.

First, her color blindness is motivated by good intentions. A lot of color-blind people mean well. They see color blindness as loving their neighbor. They see color blindness as a positive step away from being color consumed, as racist societies are by necessity. One must see color to post or comply with a WHITES ONLY sign above a drinking fountain. Color blindness advocates do not want this kind of society! Nonetheless, while color blindness can be a first step in love toward our neighbor, it is not the final step, and it can quickly become a misstep. Why? Four reasons:

1. **History is not color-blind.** "The basic assumption of color blindness is that racism has largely been defeated."[3] To invoke ethnicity/race, color blindness advocates would say, is to resurrect and perpetuate a mostly dead problem. The trouble is, while we may disagree about the extent to which we are affected by our past, the past still affects the present. And being color-blind *now* doesn't miraculously negate the effects of what happened *then* (in the past)—effects that may very well still harm your neighbor today. So, while I'm thankful for anyone who wants to treat people the same, I pray they remember that historically people have not been treated the same. I pray they remember that it is possible to show no partiality *and* keep in mind that we all have different experiences. I pray they remember that how they view and treat someone isn't how the past world, which has shaped the present world, necessarily viewed and treated someone.

2. **The world your neighbor lives in is not color-blind.**
   Your world may seem color-blind, but your neighbor's may
   be the opposite. While it sounds ideal to disregard race or
   ethnicity, color blindness can be a form of abdicating our
   responsibility to love our neighbor—something we are
   already prone to do, given our self-serving sin nature. Color
   blindness, in this sense, is quite convenient. Don't want to
   deal with race issues? Just refuse to see them. The trouble
   is, ignoring our neighbor's racial suffering may mean that
   we don't have to deal with it, but it does not mean that our
   neighbor doesn't have to deal with it. Yet to be completely
   color-blind is to blind our eyes to issues that may affect our
   neighbor. Biblical love seeks to open its eyes and see as much
   as it can as it strives to serve its neighbor and live with them
   in an understanding way. Does that mean that every time
   someone invokes race it's because the issue is actually racial?
   No, but that doesn't mean it never is, either, and given our
   society's racial history, race matters for more than it doesn't.[4]
   In short, confidently or casually declaring oneself to be color-
   blind, saying things like, "I don't see you as my black friend,
   just as my friend!" can easily sound out of touch and insensitive to those with racial wounds.
3. **Scripture is not color-blind (or gender-blind or class-
   blind).** To say that we should ignore color because of Paul's
   words in Galatians 3:28, cited above, we would then necessarily need to ignore gender if we were to consistently apply
   this text. After all, "there is no male and female." However,
   I have yet to meet a color-blindness advocate who says we
   should ignore gender. How, then, should we read this text?
   We should read it in its context.

   In Galatians, Paul was asking, "Who are the rightful heirs
   to the promises made to Abraham?"[5] Some were saying that
   you had to keep Jewish customs to be one of God's children,

which was a legalistic lie. Paul's point, then, "is that being a Jew does not make you more of an heir to the promises in Christ than being a Gentile. It is a question about standing as it relates to the inheritance, not ethnic identity full stop."[6] In other words, nothing about our identity—our gender, our class, or our ethnicity—determines our status or rank in God's kingdom. That doesn't mean we lose those parts of our identity when we become Christians, or that those parts are no longer important or real, but that those parts of our identity are not ultimate.[7] And this is what I think Dr. King was getting at in his "I Have a Dream" speech. He was not saying that ethnicity is something to be disregarded altogether; it just is not the ultimate summation of a person.[8]

Ethnicity, then, isn't something we have to shun. Rather, it's something we can celebrate, as Scripture does. We see this in Revelation 7, when all nations are still recognized in eternity, gathered around Christ's throne. This diversity highlights the unity God's people share in Christ. This diversity highlights how we are fearfully and wonderfully made, as Psalm 139:14 declares. "The consistent Christian," said civil-rights leader C. Hebert Oliver, "in head and heart also rejoices in the rich varieties of skin colors, for they too reveal the glory of God's handiwork."[9] Scripture is not color consumed on one hand or color-blind on the other. It is color-conscious.

4. **You're (likely) not as color-blind as you think you are.** Ironically, in my experience the advocates who say we should ignore race often live in neighborhoods and worship in churches where most people look just like them. But if color matters so little, why go to church or live in a neighborhood that is ethnically homogenous? One reason could be that we all tend to do what's most comfortable, and living around folks like us is most comfortable. That said, where we live

and worship can be complex choices, choices we make with Christian freedom. While we all can love comfort too much, I doubt that Samantha Lee would have said, "I will go to church only with people who look like me!" But if race has been a factor in how her community has been set up, perhaps she is more a part of a racial system than she realizes. This brings us to our next challenge for Samantha Lee.

COLOR-CONSCIOUS: A MORE EXCELLENT WAY

Color-consumed: Seeing everything through the lenses of race/ethnicity

Color-conscious: Celebrating how all people are fearfully and wonderfully made and showing no partiality while compassionately honoring different experiences

Color-blind: Ostensibly ignoring race/ethnicity

Rethinking Structural Racism

You'll recall that Samantha Lee's definition of racism is limited to feelings of animus or prejudices that we consciously hold. We can see this definition in what she asked Anna Beth: "Really—you think most cops in this country harbor prejudice in their hearts?" This is why definitions are so crucial. If that's the definition of structural racism—that everyone is really prejudiced (and therefore, to resolve this problem, everyone just needs to be kinder)—I don't agree with it either. I do think Scripture testifies that we are more sinful than we care to admit, and thus we can easily be more prejudiced than we care to admit. "The heart is deceitful above all things, and desperately sick; who can understand it?" (Jeremiah 17:9). What's more, will not sinful people create sinful cultures and systems? Did not Paul call an entire generation wicked and twisted (Philippians 2:15)? But like Samantha Lee, I don't think most people walk around actively hating others. However, I don't think that's really the point.

Theologian David Leong helps us here. He writes,

> Whenever I facilitate conversations about race, I notice that many of our initial impulses are to identify ourselves as "good people." As we react to the shameful connotations of racism, it seems that we reflexively want to defend ourselves with "I'm not a racist!" and "I'm not a judgmental person!" This impulse, while understandable, is somewhat missing the point. Rarely do I encounter a student or churchgoer who harbors an active, explicit prejudice against another racial group. But . . . if this lack of overt racism means that I'm not a racist and you're not a racist, then why is there still so much racial inequality and conflict today?[10]

While it's not the only answer, structural racism can help us understand a big part of the answer. When I say "structural racism" (what many people call "systemic" or "corporate" racism),[11] I mean an unjust system (i.e., written or unwritten laws, traditions, procedures, formal or informal habits, cultural practices) that wrongly favors an ethnic (or racial) group. Structural racism is so insidious because it can operate regardless of one's individual intentions. What's worse, even if an unjust, explicit law is removed, that doesn't mean that law doesn't still have effects. We might think of the unjust law as a match. Even if it has been blown out (that is, the law has been taken off the books), the house may very well still be on fire. I'd give Samantha Lee a historical, present, and biblical example of structural racism as I've outlined above.

First, historically, we can think of the racial segregation of Jim Crow. While laws banning integrated communities are ostensibly off the books, let's remember that Samantha Lee's neighborhood is all white. Was this only because of coincidence? Could it be that the segregation of the past (the match) has put up walls, however invisible, that remain (the ongoing fire)? Could it be the reason many Christians believe racism to be dead is because we have little to no interaction with the communities on which it has taken its toll?

Second, presently, we can think of the evil of abortion. *Abortion is a racial-justice issue.* It disproportionately affects minorities. It is entrenched in legal structures. It is state-sanctioned violence. Even Planned Parenthood of Greater New York removed Margaret Sanger's name from a clinic because of her ties to white-supremacist groups and eugenics.[12] Satan has tried to convince Christians that one should care *either* about abortion or racial justice. But what if Christians should care about *both*? If our concern for abortion does not lead us to care more about racial justice issues, I fear we are not seeing reality in all its horror. If our concern for racial justice does not lead us to care more about abortion, I fear we are not seeing reality in all its horror.

Given the bloodshed of abortion, the words of Isaiah 10 decry systemic injustices when it speaks of "decrees":

> Woe to those who decree iniquitous decrees,
>> and the writers who keep writing oppression,
> to turn aside the needy from justice
>> and to rob the poor of my people of their right,
> that widows may be their spoil,
>> and that they may make the fatherless their prey! (vv. 1–2)

And that leads me finally to a biblical example. Clearly, Scripture has in mind more than feelings when it comes to injustices that harm other image bearers. For example, in the book of Esther, when Haman codified his partiality against the Jews, soldiers had to carry out the king's edict regardless of how they *felt personally* about the Jews. While there is more going on in the story of Esther then structural ethnic partiality, there is not less. And if Samantha Lee cannot see this, she will continue to miss out on how racism divides and destroys, despite good people who individually mean well.

Avoid Making Derisive Comments

One final comment before we give Samantha Lee some positive instruction. We should end by noting that "woke" quip she texted about Anna Beth at the end of their scene. That was a cheap shot to take at her sister. It was an unfair lumping in, a broad-swiping generalization. And generalizations can easily become "slander-izations" if we're not careful. When we lump people into groups or use labels in derisive ways, we're not engaging arguments or persuading people; we're undermining them. We may very well be attacking them. And that makes our listeners defensive. And angry. And anger begets more anger. "A soft answer turns away wrath, but a harsh word stirs up anger" (Proverbs 15:1). Though he wasn't talking about race, J. I. Packer offers wise counsel about derogatorily labeling folks: "The verdict of history is that the use of prejudicial labels rules out the very possibility of charitable and constructive conversation. The interests of truth and love seem to demand that such labels be rigorously eschewed."[13]

Often labels become rhetorical weapons that are used to ostracize a point of view that bothers us. Don't like someone else's perspective? Label it, and you won't have to deal with it. In fact, the vaguer the label, the better. Labeling like this works great if our aim is simply to *denounce* one another. But if our aim is to *dialogue* with one another, we'll have to engage specific arguments rather than dismiss mere caricatures of them. With this said, we can now turn to positive instruction for Samantha Lee.

Better Questions Lead to Better Conversations

How different would Anna Beth and Samantha Lee's conversation have been if Samantha Lee hadn't stormed in the door with anger and accusation, but instead entered with sympathy and questions? Not interrogating questions, seeking mere information, but questions designed to serve her sister. What if Samantha Lee had asked,

"Hey, I noticed you didn't come to church today. What was this past week like for you?"

We can offer simple yet profound statements or questions to have better conversations about race. Here are three:

1. "Here's Where You're Right"

Imagine a conversation about race with someone you vehemently disagree with. Imagine they came in listing three to five things you were dead *right* on. Imagine a brother or sister highlighting the good points you're making. Imagine if Anna Beth had affirmed Samantha Lee in the good work she was doing and Samantha Lee had done the same for Anna Beth!

A debate can become more of a dialogue when one person leads by affirming the rightness of the other's position. We endear and win our brothers and sisters when we help them understand that we respect them, care about what they're saying, and actually do agree with them at points.

Imagine if Anna Beth and Samantha Lee, rather than jumping to defend themselves, were to sit and write out the things they *do* agree on. They might find that they have more in common than they don't. Do they agree that all people are made in God's image and therefore deserve respect, love, and justice? Yes. Do they agree that racism is evil? Yes. Do they agree that systemic racism *can* exist? Yes.

This final point could be an important revelation for them both. Anna Beth might realize that, for her sister, it's not that she doesn't believe systemic racism can exist but rather that she doesn't see evidence for its existence today. She may not see the evidence because she has a very narrow definition of systemic racism. This leads to our next category of questions.

2. "What Did You Mean by ____?"

As we'll consider later, the race conversation often feels like talking to each other at the Tower of Babel. We may be trying to build together, but we're frustrated and speaking past one another. We're using the same words but meaning different things. Clarifying what someone means before assuming what they mean will save a lot of headache and heartache. The more we disagree with someone, the more we should seek to clarify our terms as we converse with them. Otherwise, we'll assume definitions and motives and further alienate brothers, sisters, and onlookers.

3. "Does the Other Side Have Legitimate Concerns?"

There are some things Christians must agree on. Racism is bad. No Christian can disagree with that. The trouble is, while God has spoken clearly, he has not spoken exhaustively about everything, racial issues included.[14] That means that we can have legitimately different viewpoints on some things and still be Christians. If we can recognize that different sides of an issue likely have valid points, rather than demonize one another for holding those points, we may make some progress, by God's grace. But if we don't start showing some sympathy in a way that our dialogue partner would recognize as sympathy—if we keep coming into these conversations with generalizations and assumptions—we will continue to sound like Anna Beth and Samantha Lee.

Youth and Elderly, Take Note

We're out of time for this counseling session, but Anna Beth and Samantha Lee both have things to think about and work on, and we'll pray they both have years to do so, since they're both relatively young. And that's yet another reason racial matters are so hard to talk about—often we're speaking like young people do. Overconfident. Untested. Unnuanced. Uncharitable. Have you ever noticed how people with gray hair seem so magnanimous in conversations with people with whom they vehemently disagree? That doesn't mean you can't find an old fool. But it's more likely for a young person to speak foolishly than an older one. Think of Ruth Bader Ginsburg and Antonin Scalia, of Robert George and Cornel West, of John Piper and Wayne Grudem—all of them had major disagreements, all of them modeled how to handle them charitably. We who are younger would do well to take note.

But the youth are not the only ones who need to get out their notebooks. What the youth do bring to the table is a certain zeal, an enthusiasm, a fire. Just because one is aged doesn't mean they get everything right and the younger generation gets everything wrong. How many old people are wrongly stuck in their ways or in the perspectives and traditions they grew up with? The younger generation is not wrong for seeking to live just lives, nor should they be made to feel badly for doing so. But that's enough for now. We need to turn to Eun-ji, who has an important perspective in our story.

Questions for Reflection and Discussion (for Samantha Lee)

1. Would you have counseled Samantha Lee differently than I? Why? In what ways? From which passages of Scripture?
2. What questions/statements have you found to help clarify and advance conversations about racial issues? What questions/statements have you found to hinder them?

CHAPTER 5

A MINORITY MASK—
MEET JANE (EUN-JI)

Hope deferred makes the heart sick.

—PROVERBS 13:12

No matter how long you've been here, you're always seen as different and foreign. People are always asking you where you're from, and it leads to an ongoing sense of marginalization.

—DUKE KWON[1]

On Monday morning Jane was feeling nervous. Today was her first day at her new job, and she didn't know a soul. She'd spoken briefly to her boss, Samantha, but they'd never met in person. Not for lack of trying. During the phone call in which Jane had been offered and had accepted this job, it had somehow come up that Jane was a Christian, and Samantha had invited her to check out her church. Jane took Samantha up on her offer—in part hoping to find a new church home and in part hoping to run into her new boss so she'd have a familiar face this morning. But that hadn't happened. Samantha had texted her an apology at the last minute, saying she couldn't meet. Regardless, Jane had attended the prayer meeting and the main service at Lincoln Ridge Bible Church alone.

Here she was, alone again, this time sitting in the front office, anxiously waiting to meet her new work team and be shown to her desk.

The door opened, and Jane stood and looked up with what she hoped was an enthusiastic smile. "Hi, Samantha!" she exclaimed.

"Oh, sweetheart, I'm from the South—it's Samantha Lee," the woman responded, giving a generous wink and a big smile.

Jane heard Samantha's unspoken message loud and clear: (1) she was the boss, and (2) botching her name was a transgression not to be repeated. "I'm so sorry," Jane said, blushing.

"No worries! I'm sorry I couldn't meet you yesterday at church; I had a family emergency. You must be Jane," Samantha Lee said.

This was Jane's American name, not her birth name. As a little girl, she had picked it because of a book she saw at a library once—*Jane Eyre*. The book's cover was pretty. Jane wanted to be pretty. And so Jane it was, despite her real name being Eun-ji. But no one, save her Korean family and friends, could say that. Eun-ji knew that from awkward conversation after awkward conversation about how to pronounce her name. And she wasn't about to tutor her boss, whom she already felt she had dishonored. Therefore Eun-ji must be Jane, out of deference, if not necessity.

"Yes, yes," Jane answered quickly, speedily doing the mental calculus about her names. By this point in her life, such math was easy, even subconscious.

"Great! And where are you from?" Samantha Lee responded with genuine curiosity, unable to tell exactly what ethnicity Jane was.

The question. *"Where are you from?"*

It was a seemingly insignificant thing—Jane being asked that question—but a stinging one nevertheless. Given that she had been asked it her entire life, Jane had long ago internalized this message: *I must not belong. I must not be from here.*

"California. Bay Area," Jane said quickly, respectfully, confidently. "Well, I should say I grew up there, but I'm originally from—"

A crash interrupted Jane.

The bank's maintenance man had dropped his toolbox from the top of the ladder he stood on. He had a sign in one hand that he was clearly tasked to hang in the bank's main entrance. Trying not to drop it from the position he was holding it in, he asked Jane for help.

"Ma'am, would you mind sliding that box over to the bottom of the ladder just so it's out of the way?" he asked Jane politely from atop the ladder.

"Oh—sure, of course," Jane said, walking over and kneeling down to move the box. Jane stood back up and found her original footing next to her boss, who was studying the sign. Jane looked at it as well.

Black Lives Matter, it read.

Jane noticed that a frown crossed Samantha Lee's face. What Jane didn't know was that that simple sign sparked a memory in Samantha Lee's mind—a time when she and Anna Beth had talked. Or debated. Or argued.

"How can you support Black Lives Matter?" Samantha Lee had shouted at her little sister in the heat of battle. *"Have you even read their website? They're advancing the LGBT agenda! They're anarchists!"*

Remembering she was at work, Samantha Lee regained her composure, looked at her new employee, and wondered what she might be thinking.

She couldn't tell.

"We can talk briefly about the bank's position on social issues first, if that would help," Samantha Lee said, smiling uncomfortably in an attempt to break the ice. "Let's go up to my office, Jane."

Without saying a word, Jane politely nodded and followed her new boss's lead.

As they boarded the elevator, Jane couldn't help but think about it. It was clear from watching her white boss looking at a Black Lives Matter sign, as well as from the word of hope she had heard at church on Sunday, that the black-white dynamic is what mattered most. Black people said as much. White people said as much.

Of course Jane didn't want to be dismissive toward the sensitivity and necessity of the black-white conversation. Given the nation's history and present moment, it was vital to have this conversation. Malachi Brewers was dead. Killed. Murdered maybe, after all. And this made Jane so sad.

Yet what also saddened Jane was what she had been told lots of times: the black-white conversation needed to be addressed first to create space for other minority voices. That's what a black pastor had told her at her old church, the one she had attended before moving to Philadelphia.

Jane would never forget that conversation. She remembered how much courage she had to muster even to ask her old pastor for that conversation. Since childhood, Jane had been taught not to question authority, to listen and not speak when in the presence of an elder. She had been taught to avoid asking for help, lest she be a burden. Hence, positioning for any kind of visibility—speaking up when not spoken to—felt so arrogant, so wrong to her. But the conversation about race had been growing in importance at her old church. She thought her experiences could add a helpful perspective for all of Christ's multiethnic bride. She understood racial matters mattered, and she wanted the church to better reflect the power of the gospel. So Jane chose Christ over comfort. She decided to open up.

And she was shut down. "We're just getting this conversation started at our church," Jane's old pastor had told her. "We really just need to focus on the black-and-white conversation for now."

Yet "now" soon became forever, and the black-white conversation never broadened to include other ethnicities. Jane began to notice that when people talked about "diversity," they would associate it solely with "African American." Want a diverse office? Have more black people in it. A diverse church? Put more black people up front. All the while, Jane was left feeling irrelevant. Invisible. Her legitimate concerns were trivialized and isolated because they didn't fit into the historic conflict between blacks and whites. Jane—Eun-ji—was a puzzle piece people weren't sure what to do with. Like most puzzles, people seemed to want to do the edges first—and only then fill in the rest. It had been this way her whole life, she realized.

Jane was a second-generation Korean American. Her parents had moved from Korea to Los Angeles, where Jane was born. But when the race riots broke out, they had moved to San Francisco, where Jane had lots of relatives whom she enjoyed. And a Korean church she enjoyed.

Until her parents had gotten divorced, that is. When they did, Jane had moved with her mom to Georgia, which she did not enjoy. There Jane had watched her mom deal with the pressure to assimilate to the predominantly white culture they found themselves in. There Eun-ji had no space to learn what it meant to be Korean.

Instead, as she grew up, Jane wrestled with shame over her Asian heritage. After all, she was fetishized. She was always made to feel like a foreigner. Her ethnicity was a game of whack-a-mole to most people: "So, if you're not Chinese, are you Japanese?" Her success in life was used by some white people as the standard to show that black people could also succeed if they just tried hard enough.

Black people. Jane's parents struggled with them, to say the least. As a child, she was too young to see why. Her parents never told her explicitly. And Jane would never dare ask them. But over the years, Jane could piece together, from passing comments here and there, that when the race riots got bad in LA, the hostility wasn't between her parents and white people. It was between them and black people. As far as Jane's parents were concerned, blacks looted her dad's store during the riots. Blacks spray-painted vulgar graffiti—CHINK LAND—on the salon where her mom worked. That's why they moved to the Bay Area.

But Jane couldn't tell her story at church. There, she was voiceless.

Sure, Asians may not have a unified story, but the bigger issue was feeling like she was not allowed to speak "out of order." She had to come second to the black-white polarity. She reminded herself— preached to herself—again, "Eun-ji, you can benefit from more teaching on the black-white conversation." It took some work on her own heart for her to feel like she could say that, but again, she honestly recognized there needed to be more teaching on that conversation. It was a historically unique conversation. Black lives didn't matter enough to people, and Jane would be the first to genuinely say so. Jane honestly didn't want to compete with other minorities for a seat at the table.

She just wanted to sit alongside them.

She wasn't asking to take over the conversation.

She was asking if whites and blacks would share it. Or was her role simply to defer again?

The elevator's ding snapped Jane out of her thoughts. They had reached the floor where her boss's office was and where her new office would be, too, for that matter.

"Whatcha thinking about over there?" Samantha Lee asked kindly as they stepped out of the elevator.

"Oh, uh—nothing," Jane responded with an endearing smile.

"I really am jealous you grew up in California." Samantha Lee said. And not being able to hold it in anymore, she went for it. She knew she was at work. She knew she was the boss. But at the prayer service, her pastor had talked about being willing to take a risk in conversations about race. So risk she did.

"Hey, I know this is awkward and I probably shouldn't ask this as your boss, and I know you said you're from California, but . . . where are you *from?*"

Jane was surprised and completely unsurprised. She gave her scripted response, "My parents are from Korea, I grew up in California," and so on, and this answer seemed to satisfy Samantha Lee's curiosities. Jane and her boss got back to work easily enough.

Jane's onboarding was largely uneventful. She signed some papers, asked some clarifying questions. Jane was brought in to fill a new position, so she had some questions about what her role would be, but Samantha Lee gave her every assurance they'd figure it out.

"Don't worry," she said with cheerful confidence. "You're on the bus, and we'll find the right seat for you."

It was all standard fare, really. When they had finished their orientation, Samantha Lee showed Jane to her new desk, a cute cubicle, smack in the middle of the office. Jane noticed that, given the layout of the offices, her colleagues literally surrounded her on every side. Most were white, and a few were black. Jane didn't feel one way or the other about all of this. As a minority, she knew what it was like to be sprinkled among white people. Jane just felt eager to sit down, set up shop, and have a moment to herself.

"Wait!" Samantha Lee said with excitement. "Let me first give you a tour of the office real quick and introduce you to everyone. You're going to *love* these folks."

That's right, Eun-ji thought to herself. *Black and white edges of the puzzle first.*

Nonetheless, from what Jane could tell on first impression, her boss was right. Her colleagues all seemed like great people. The ladies ended their tour, and Jane came back to her desk to find a big welcome basket. Candy and flowers shot out of it like fireworks. Samantha Lee smiled and left Jane to officially start her day. Finally by herself, Jane sat down, took a breath, and began trying to figure out her new role.

Questions for Reflection and Discussion

1. At what points did you resonate with Jane's story?
2. What does Jane get right? What does she get wrong?
3. Describe the mask Jane is wearing and who she is hiding from. (Hint: she's hiding from more than one person.)
4. Should the race conversation be primarily black and white? Why or why not? Which passages of Scripture inform your answer?
5. On the scale of 1 to 10 below, how important is your race/ethnicity to your identity as a Christian?

1	2	3	4	5	6	7	8	9	10

Not Important   Very Important

6. What parts of this chapter challenged or bothered you?
7. Do you pray for people like Jane in your life? Why or why not?

ENCOURAGEMENT FOR JANE

Do nothing from selfish ambition or conceit, but in humility count others more significant than yourselves. Let each of you look not only to his own interests, but also to the interests of others.

—PHILIPPIANS 2:3-4

We should all be checking preferences at the door to better love and serve our brothers and sisters in Christ.

—TIM CHIANG[1]

You'll remember that Jane had just moved to the area and was considering whether she should join LRBC. In light of her struggles and thoughts, here's the pastoral counsel I would give her. First, I'd commend her humility.

Jane displayed a deeply Christian resiliency in fighting self-interest. Recall how she recognized the importance of the black-white conversation. *Malachi Brewers was dead*, she thought to herself. Recall how she preached to herself that she could learn from the black-white conversation. In doing so, Jane acknowledged that her story wasn't the only story. She put others' needs before her own, which was Christ-like of her. She could have insisted that one had to choose the black-white conversation or a broader conversation, but she didn't. Jane didn't even deny the uniqueness of the black-white conversation.

The Black-White Conversation Is Unique

Historically, Asians and blacks simply have not been treated the exact same way in America, and the latter group's struggle with whites and notions of race in this country do predate the former group's struggle. This is what arguments that essentially say, "Asian Americans overcame great obstacles—prejudice, internment camps in some cases—so why can't blacks?" fail to realize. A simplistic one-to-one comparison shouldn't be drawn between one minority group that was enslaved for more than two centuries and another that wasn't, even if we can all agree that both of their experiences were extraordinarily difficult. Such comparisons don't take into account how the notions of race surrounding one group were used to perpetuate claims about another. Jane recognized that.

It's okay and helpful to look at the unique chasm between blacks and whites historically. Jane was simply asking that this not be the only thing we look at. And you know what? She's right. That's what I'd say to her: "You're right!"

The Black-White Conversation Is Limited

In our desire to have one conversation—however unique and important it may be—black and white Christians can too easily exclude or dismiss other conversations about different ethnicities' struggles. If Jesus did indeed die for people from every tribe, tongue, and nation, we should happily and humbly hear from every tribe, tongue, and nation. This will be hard to do, however, if we only have conversations about race once every blue moon in our churches. Could it be that we need more conversations, not fewer?

After all, even how I've talked about the Asian American struggle so far makes it sound as if there is one, singular struggle that Asian Americans face. Though many Asian Americans may face similar struggles, being Asian, or even Asian American, is not a monolithic experience. I'm embarrassed to write such an obvious statement, but I've needed reminding of it, and maybe you do too: Asia is a really big continent; it's not one place. America, too, is really big.

That means, when it comes to talking about or with our Asian brothers and sisters, we can be talking about vastly different experiences, even different experiences within the same cultures. The experience of a second- or third-generation Asian American may very well be different than that of being a first-generation Asian American, and second- and third-generation Asian Americans can feel that difference. They can often feel as "third-culture people, belonging neither to the white-majority culture nor the Asian-immigrant culture."[2] Indeed, behind the label "Asian" is a beautiful, vast diversity. Cambodians may live and experience life differently than Vietnamese, and these experiences and lifestyles can differ from those of Koreans. If we treat the black-and-white divide as the only divide that needs racial reconciliation—whatever we may mean by that—we will neglect the opportunity to minister to other divides that may be facing our nonblack and nonwhite brothers and sisters, divides that have little to do with black and white. For instance, we could talk about the divides between Koreans and Japanese; we could talk about the poverty rates of Bhutanese Americans as compared to other Asian American populations, and we could keep going. But all of this goes to say that to focus only on the black-and-white divide, then, is to think about racial reconciliation too narrowly. And in light of all this, I'd thank Jane.

I'd thank her for reminding me about the diversity of Christ's bride. I'd thank her for educating me about different struggles. As a Christian who is also African American, I've been humbled and helped when my Asian brothers and sisters tell me about their challenges. In sharing their struggles, they haven't taken away from my struggles; they've put them in perspective. In sharing their struggles, my Asian brothers and sisters haven't hindered my view of God's people—they've enhanced it. They've shined a light on a God who has preserved and kept *all* his children through many dangers, toils, and snares. So I'd thank Jane, and thank God for his gift to me in this sister challenging me to think more broadly. Jane's role isn't just to serve the black-white conversation by being a bridge between the two sides, however effective she may be in doing that good work. Brothers and sisters like Jane are themselves gifts for the rest of Christ's bride to cherish and listen to.

Churches Are Imperfect

Third, I'd lament with Jane.[3] I'd grieve the challenges she mentioned in her story—and those of different Asian brothers and sisters. Jane's story highlights the horror of how various groups of Asians have been made to seek respect and acceptance from broader American society. Her story highlights how Asian brothers and sisters have worked hard or served in wars to show that they, too, were American—even if doing so meant sharing in part of the responsibility of propagating the model-minority myth. And while I cannot relate to that specific struggle, I can relate to the general struggle of wanting to belong. We all can relate. What we see in Jane's story is not only the Asian struggle to be seen as American—hard as that struggle is. We also see the very real and human yearning for belonging. For having a place. This desire, it seems, has been baked into human nature. It is not good for us to be alone (Genesis 2:18). People yearn for a community, a home.

Jane teaches us the importance of praying and working so that all church members feel like they have a *home* in our churches. After all, before Jane is Asian, or before I am black, or before you—reader—are what you are, you are a Christian. And this is our most fundamental identity, children of the household of faith (Ephesians 2:19). So in counseling Jane, I'd gently encourage her to remember our shared identity in Christ. I'd gently encourage her to remember that despite the world's making her earn her place for its affection, her identity and value are not ultimately found in being an American, a woman, or an Asian. It's found in Jesus. All else is rubbish compared to Jesus.

Now, Jesus's followers will forget this truth at times. No doubt, members of the church will, at times, sin against Jane. We grieve this—that Christians aren't always humble. We should grieve how we nitpick and bicker and can do so in racially insensitive ways. We should call out those sins. That said, if Jane never wants to be sinned against, I'd tell her that she shouldn't join LRBC, or any church for that matter.

But then I'd tell her that, unlike the world, LRBC and many other churches are full of Christians who *repent* of such sins. We're full of people who recognize that none of us belong around the Lord's table, but because of God's mercy, we all have a seat. We can't say to one, "You sit here in a good place," while we say to the other, "You stand over there." Such partiality fails to uphold the royal law of Scripture: "You shall love your neighbor as yourself" (James 2:1–13).

Remember Where Your Identity Lies

Why would I say all of this to Jane? Why would I go on about her identity? I'd highlight her most fundamental identity so that she doesn't feel that we see her primarily as Asian. I'd highlight her truest identity so she doesn't say, "Hey, since you guys see me first and foremost as Asian, you must address my Asian-ness if you're going to address me." In other words, I don't want her to feel that until we're addressing issues that touch on Asians, we haven't addressed her at all.

To be clear, I wouldn't be saying to Jane that we're going to ignore altogether how the Lord has made her, lest we be color-blind (as we've already addressed in Samantha Lee's encouragement). Far from it! As has been said, we should seek for brothers and sisters like Jane to teach us more, not less, about their experiences. We should praise God for how multiethnic his bride is and how he has made each member of it. We should rejoice in the kaleidoscope of skin colors he has redeemed. Jane is a full member of God's multiethnic choir. We should sing like that's true. We should lament like that's true. We should speak like that's true. But we can't do this with Jane if she feels, *or if we make her to feel*, as if her being Asian is the sum total of who she is, because that teaches her to find her identity where the world is telling her to find it—in something other than Jesus.

Understanding that she, like everyone else, is more than her ethnicity will help Jane in her conversations about race. For instance, if she sees people as the sum total of their ethnicity or race, she might simply see Samantha Lee as ignorant and white—period. But if she understands that there is more to Samantha Lee, and that as sisters in Christ they share more in common than Jane does with a non-Christian who happens to be Asian, their conversations can change. Very practically, when Samantha Lee asks, "Where are you from?" Jane could hear that as just another microaggression. Or she could assume the best. She could believe that Samantha Lee isn't just an exemplar of ignorant white people but is her sister who is truly striving to learn. She could respond graciously to the question—with excitement even—as she has the opportunity to educate someone. She could extend goodwill rather than pull back in suspicion. She could hear a better word than Samantha Lee even spoke. Ultimately, Jane could overlook the offense (Proverbs 19:11). Remembering that her ethnicity is not the sum total of who she is can help her do that.

"So, I hear you on the need to have a more diverse conversation than black and white," I'd tell Jane. "But don't wait until someone at your church is addressing Asians to feel like we're addressing you.

When your pastor preaches the gospel, he's addressing you. When fellow church members speak truth about what Christians do or shouldn't do, they're addressing you. When they sing psalms and hymns and spiritual songs to one another, they're addressing you—the you that is clothed in the righteousness of Jesus."

And I'd tell the same thing to every member of the church, whether they be in the ethnic minority or majority. As two ethnic minorities, Jane and I could probably relate to how we have to preach these truths to ourselves, given that our ethnicity is often obvious by virtue of our being in the minority. Yet white brothers and sisters need to hear these truths as well, especially if they're in the racial majority. They need to hear these truths not only because white brothers and sisters are not a-cultural or a-ethnic, but also because being in the racial majority means you will face a greater temptation to ignore other peoples' experiences and remain within your comfort zone. The truth is, all members of the church should feel that we're giving up something when we gather as a church. Whether it is our music preferences or our cultural comforts, all of us should be laying down our preferences in service to one another. The good question Jane is pushing us to ask is, *are we really doing that?*

Such a question should cause us to take a good, long look in the mirror and examine what we find most comfortable at our churches, compared to what other ethnic groups find. Such a question also brings up a challenging fact: every church has a predominant culture. This may sound contrary to all I've just said, but I don't think it is. Yes, the church should be a place where everyone is laying down their preferences, but it's also true that some preferences, customs, and practices have to be largely agreed upon for the sake of order (1 Corinthians 14:40). Your church likely has a certain style of music, for instance, however diverse it may be. And this is a fine thing. If the style changed every week—"Next week is country week!"—that would make the style of the music the point rather than the content—and the content should be Jesus. He's the point.

So, in short, if a church is predominantly Korean or predominantly white or predominantly Kenyan or predominantly black, Chinese, or some other ethnicity—it will have a certain culture to it. There's no use in pretending our churches aren't what they are. In fact, to do otherwise, to act as if your church is a-cultural, is false advertising. Ethnic minorities in any church will be confronted with the fact that being in the ethnic minority means that being at the church will be harder for them than for those in the majority. And those in the ethnic majority must keep this difference in difficulty in mind. How much compassion could be built in churches if we simply remembered that those in the ethnic minority can easily have harder struggles than those in the majority? Praise God for brothers and sisters like Jane who give up a lot for the sake of Christ, even when it comes to talking about race, to be at churches where they are in the minority.

One Last Note: Headlights Not Taillights

Jane couldn't hear Samantha Lee's argument with Anna Beth about Black Lives Matter, but we did. Remember what Samantha Lee thought when she saw the BLM sign being hung at work? We'd be remiss not to address it.

Again, we should train our instincts to highlight evidences of grace. Samantha Lee means to stand for the truths and principles of God's Word, however unpopular they may sound. She means to stand for what God's Word says about sexuality, and there are Christians who could learn from her courage. Taking such a stand will only be more difficult in the coming days.

However, Samantha Lee went on to make a sweeping statement about Black Lives Matter. Critiquing the organization highlights a common, well-intended but misguided instinct of some evangelicals: we spend more energy condemning organizations and philosophies that seek to confront racism than we do condemning racism itself.

Beloved, if we don't like what someone or some group is saying about racism, let's put forward a better way. Yet we often seem to only critique. We often seem more troubled by the *accusation* of racism than the *presence* of racism—and it is this defensive impulse the led Martin Luther King Jr. to say that American churches are too often the taillight and not the headlight.[4] That is, we're too often found reacting to evils like racism rather than proactively leading against them. And other voices have stepped in to fill the void.

I'm not saying that there aren't valid criticisms to be made of an organization like BLM; in the next chapter we'll consider how the pastor especially is to defend the sheep from false ideologies. That said, I think the more challenging question for us evangelicals to ask is not what is or isn't wrong with Black Lives Matter, but what are we doing to combat racism?

Conclusion

Jane's story tells us about the importance of listening to more than our own story. In light of this, there are two conversational prompts that we can take away to improve our communications about race and racism:

1. **"Could you please share your experience?"** Showing sincere interest in someone else's experience regarding race can be far more powerful than we might assume. The listener can feel seen and heard, validated and valued. When we ask to hear others' stories, we show that we realize our story isn't

the only one. What's more, the conversation shifts from being about abstract arguments to something personal, something we can't really argue against. So set up a time to talk. Make clear what you'd like to talk about and see if the other person is willing to speak. And instead of coming with twenty questions, come with this following one.

2. **"Could I please share my experience with you?"** At her old church, Jane took a step of courage by offering to share her experience. In sharing her story, she was offering to share a part of herself that could aid that church in building faith, unity, and love. Offering to share as Jane did is also a winsome way to gain a hearing. One could lob a grenade and simply start a fight, or one could humbly request to take the conversation to a deeper level. Asking to share our experiences can be a disarming way to convey some of the matters dearest to us. Vulnerability builds trust.

Questions for Reflection and Discussion

1. Do your conversations about race usually wind up being about the black-white divide only, or are they more expansive? Why?

2. How can we make our conversations about racial matters more inclusive, and why should we?

3. Why should Christians remember our shared identity in Christ? What happens if we don't? Why is this identity hard to remember?

4. How can Christians keep the emphasis on our shared identity in Christ in our conversations about race? How can we do so without sounding like we're denigrating the experiences of others?

CHAPTER 6

A MAN AMONG MASKS—
MEET THEIR PASTOR

Shepherd the flock of God that is among you . . .
eagerly.

—1 PETER 5:2

When do we become morally culpable, especially
as pastors, for an ignorance of our history?

—JONATHAN LEEMAN[1]

It's Monday morning, the morning countless pastors feel empty. Discouraged. Spiritually hungover. Blue.

Rev. Bruce Johnson, pastor of Lincoln Ridge Bible Church, had learned long ago not to take Monday morning off. He was at his worst those mornings, and he refused to make his family endure it. The church could pay for this time. He'd take another day to compensate for his weekend's work.

So, at his computer Bruce sat—catching up on emails from the last few days. Of course, there were the normal notes folks sent. Some picking nits about the sermon he had labored over. A couple others offering sincere encouragements. All of this would aid the

Monday morning quarterbacking Bruce would do in an hour or so, however hard he'd try not to. Such was the weekly cycle—a mountaintop on Sunday, the wilderness on Monday.

And the wilderness would be especially treacherous today. Bruce knew a couple of bombs awaited him in his inbox. He had skimmed one Sunday morning before the prayer service. Typically he wouldn't have checked his email right before the church gathered. It would only distract him. He knew better. Plus, Darius was going to show up any minute, so the two of them could review his word of hope. But Darius hadn't shown up yet, and Bruce couldn't resist.

There was so much going on that week with Malachi Brewers. And the subject line of one email was just too enticing. Or painful. Or shocking. It was from José Luis—a brother he loved, a brother he struggled with. Bruce knew that as a white man, he could easily speak about this past week poorly. Maybe this email would help him not to do that at the prayer service.

So he grabbed his mouse and hovered over José's unopened note. *Click.*

José Luis <Luis.Jose@mail.com>
To: Pastor <pastorbruce@LRBC.mail>
Subject: We're Leaving LRBC
Date: October 4, 2020

Pastor Bruce,

I write you with sympathy and caution. Sympathy, because I know your task as a shepherd isn't an easy one. I don't envy you. Caution, because my wife and I can no longer sit under the pastors at LRBC, and so out of care for our own souls, we're leaving (Proverbs 4:23). Allow me to explain.

You know my wife. You know as a biracial woman, both white and black, this world is especially hard for her, especially with weeks like the past one. She's too white for some black people, too black for some white people. However, with strength she's navigated this painful spectrum. I'm thankful her parents instilled in her—ever since she was a little girl—that she was beloved by God. They spoke to her about both sides of her heritage. As a kid, she ate baked mac-and-cheese and Kraft too. What's more, her parents helped her understand that Jesus knows her better than she knows herself. She might not have had it at her predominantly white school, but she had pockets, like her family, where she was known and loved.

But we find ourselves too often asking, "Where is our family?" at LRBC. When it comes to racial justice, our "brothers and sisters" have not shown up for us. The fathers of LRBC, you pastors, don't lead out on these issues. By this point, my wife knows what to expect on Sunday mornings after racial tragedies. She'll show up, and from the other women of the church, she'll get a casual, "Hey! How was your week?" Someone is more likely to ask to touch her hair than ask how she's doing with the news of Malachi Brewers.

No one has reached out to her.

My wife's heart has cracked on two sides—a white crack for white people who are ignorant. A black crack for black people who are oppressed. And you all have left her to figure this out on her own because either you don't notice or don't care. Both are problems for us. Pastor, if we don't address these issues head-on, is it any wonder why minorities think Christianity is a white man's religion—if it only addresses the concerns of white people?

Let me turn to myself now, since I don't intend to speak only for my wife.

Me. You know me. You know I'm Mexican. You heard what President Trump said about my people. And yet you've said nothing while church members celebrate him. Some days I leave service feeling like our church is filled with a bunch of racists. So we're leaving in search of more compassionate pastures and pastors. I know we've had our struggles. I know you're praying about these matters. But white pastor, we need more than prayer, though we will pray for you.

Grace and peace,
José Luis, for the Ramirez Family

"Leaving?" Bruce muttered to himself that Sunday morning when he first read José Luis's email. He was crushed. He so wanted the diversity of the church to increase. Despite any rough patches he had with José Luis, he wanted him to stay—badly!

But José Luis's email had been sent. Bruce wondered if José Luis had bcc'd anyone else at the church on it. He knew some would hear the email as José Luis leaving the faith. Even Darius was worried about José Luis's trajectory, and—

"Shoot!" Bruce said to himself. There he sat, thinking, while the prayer meeting was about to begin, and Bruce still hadn't seen Darius. Pastor Bruce shot up and sped to find him. So began Sunday morning.

But it was Monday now, the wilderness. Bruce marked José Luis's email unread—again. He needed to think about it more before responding, not that he didn't have a draft in his mind already. He had started formulating it the second he had finished reading the message.

On to the next email, this one from Brother Mack. Bruce guessed what he might say. Bracing himself, Bruce moved his mouse over the unopened note. It was funny to Bruce how, oddly enough, the mouse was free. He was the one who felt trapped. On one side were the likes of Brother Mack, on the other, the likes of his daughter—and these were just two of the sides surrounding him. But now was the time for clearing the inbox, not analyzing it. So Bruce moved toward Brother Mack's unread note.

Click.

George Mack <George.Mack@mail.com>
To: Pastor <pastorbruce@LRBC.mail>
Subject: Inconsistency
Date: October 5, 2020

Pastor,

While I'm generally grateful for your leadership, I have questions about yesterday's prayer service. Particularly the lament over the Malachi Brewers case, which has yet to be resolved or even litigated. And yet we lament? Where is the lament over abortion? Over rioting? Why the selective lament?

I am honestly not upset we're lamenting, but I am not looking for political spins on Sunday. In fact, I don't want any politics on my Lord's Day. I can check the news for politics. I'd encourage you just to keep preaching the gospel rather than steer our church toward overemphasizing one sin the culture is currently fascinated with. Thanks for hearing this out. I look forward to your response.

Best,
Brother Mack

"Yep," Bruce said to himself, shaking his head, "just as I thought."
Bruce was right, and sad that he was. A memory flashed into Bruce's
mind—a time when he tried to confront Brother Mack about some
racial blind spots.

"You kidding me, pastor?!" Bruce remembered Brother Mack saying to him, with the volume up. *"I don't have a racist bone in my body!"*
Brother Mack said angrily. Coming back to the present, Bruce was
sure he wasn't eager for another meeting like that.

But he also wanted to maintain the unity of the church. He
wanted the unity to increase! He didn't want to lose people like
Brother Mack; he wanted to help them. That's why, in the past,
Bruce's strategy had been to hunker down and wait out the news
surrounding high-profile racial shootings. Then the surrounding
tensions could blow over. Then his people could hear better. After all,
people like Brother Mack meant well. They could be reasoned with,
Bruce figured, though that didn't make them any easier to deal with.

Doing the pastoral calculations in his head, Bruce took a breath
and took heart. He knew these Monday emails, especially Brother
Mack's, didn't speak for most of the church. Most of the church
loved and supported their pastor and one another. Most of the
church genuinely wanted to grow in racial reconciliation and their
understanding of these matters.

Which meant he needed to do something to spur on that
growth.

Bruce had begun suspecting that his church's lack of diversity was connected, in no small way, to his lack of intentionality
in pursuing it. Brothers like Darius helped him see that, and this
insight was humbling. Bruce realized he hadn't been praying for,
discipling, or training leaders with diversity in mind. It wasn't that
Pastor Bruce didn't want to. He just hadn't really thought about it
in his day-to-day ministry.

But now he was thinking. *Should I hire some people of color? Should
I bring in a black preacher for Martin Luther King Jr. weekend?*

Bruce wasn't sure. In fact, if he was honest, he would say he was just dipping his toes into this racial reconciliation stuff. Darius's word of hope was the first of its kind for his church, and it was a hit. He hoped Darius, and members like him, were heartened by seeing the church take a step forward, however clumsily. But it was the best foot Bruce knew how to put forward. After all, he hadn't studied anything about race in seminary. No classes on the church and race relations were offered, or any courses on a theology of ethnicity and its implications, past or present. No seminars on the history of the black church—at least, no seminar he was required to take. Studying racial justice was a nice-to have, not a need-to-have—one reserved for those who were passionate about it. And those students' passions were regularly under the scrutiny of a lot of Bruce's classmates.

But that was beside the point. The question Bruce asked himself was how he could teach about these matters he hadn't been taught on. And yet that's what everyone seemed to want him to do. Everyone was asking for the church to *do* something—which really meant everyone was asking *him* to do something. The criticisms in this conversation felt endless; the clear solutions felt sparse.

But something had to change.

Even the deacons were struggling with this conversation. How could the church talk about these matters if its leaders couldn't? Burying his face in his hands, Pastor Johnson felt overwhelmed.

He began to pray.

He prayed with thanks for the apparent diversity the church enjoyed, however little of it was left. It looked good up front, Darius up there and all. But he prayed with anxiety because he knew behind closed doors and on social media it was a different story. He knew his members attacked each other on Facebook. He prayed with confusion because he had heard some of the books other members were reading about racial justice. These books seemed to say some good things but some pretty bad things too.

As he was praying, Bruce's phone pinged with a notification. Another email just came in. A church member was recommending the church start a book study on race. Sighing, Bruce clicked the link to check out the book. He scanned the description, feeling sympathetic but cautious.

Questions for Reflection and Discussion

1. How does Jesus feel about churches like Pastor Bruce's? How should we?
2. At what points did you resonate with Bruce's story?
3. What does Bruce get right? What does he get wrong?
4. Describe the mask Bruce is wearing and who all he is hiding from. (Hint: he's hiding from more than one person.)
5. Is letting the news of racial tragedies "blow over" a wise pastoral strategy? Why or why not? Which passages of Scripture inform your answer?
6. Is Pastor Bruce wrong to be suspicious of the books suggested to him? Why or why not? Which passages of Scripture inform your answer?
7. Do you regularly pray for your pastor as he shepherds your fellow church members amid race relations? Why or why not?

ENCOURAGEMENT FOR THEIR PASTOR

Exhort and rebuke with all authority. Let no one disregard you.

—TITUS 2:15

Pastors, there are a lot of things we should do. There are a lot of things we could do. But never underestimate the power of a strong pulpit.

—CAMERON TRIGGS[1]

What can we say to encourage Bruce and pastors like him, who are dipping their toes into racial matters as they lead their congregations? We could ask why they're just now dipping in their toes. Have their churches been unwilling to have this conversation? Have they, as pastors, been unwilling to have this conversation? What's that unwillingness symptomatic of? Maybe these pastors aren't sure how to have this conversation. Maybe they didn't know they needed to have it until very recently. Whatever their reasons, they're considering the conversation now, and that is something to praise God for. Let's say I'm a fellow pastor at a different church, with whom Bruce is good friends, and he reaches out to me for counsel after the emails he's received and the weekend he's had. Here's the general encouragement I'd give him.

Do What You Can and Trust God

Do everything you can, and trust God with the results. As pastors, we are in jobs that we are, by definition, insufficient to carry out—and shepherding our flock amid racial tensions, strife, or injustice only highlights our weakness that much more. What shall we do? Set our hope on God, for he will deliver us (2 Corinthians 1:10); trust in him with all our hearts, lean not on our own understanding, acknowledge him, and he will make our paths straight (Proverbs 3:5–6); and keep a close watch on ourselves and on the teaching, persist in this, for by doing so we will save both ourselves and our hearers (1 Timothy 4:16). Brothers, it's okay not to know what to do next all the time. The Lord knows, and he will make it clear.

Don't Underestimate What We're Up Against

The letter Pastor Bruce received from José Luis was discouraging, but it also can help Pastor Bruce grow. First, it reminds me that as pastors try to follow Jesus amid race relations and lead our people to do the same, we're up against a lot. No doubt, we are engaged in warfare with the Enemy (Ephesians 6:10–18). But on top of that, we're up against churches and a nation that have been historically and painfully divided. We're up against de jure segregation that was pervasive and de facto segregation that is persistent. When it comes to our congregations and the diversity of them, we have responsibility, to be sure. But that responsibility pales in comparison to the forces we're up against, forces outside our control. As pastors, we're dealing with *people*—people who are already finnicky beings, and on top of that, they come and they go. We're dealing with neighborhoods that shift and change, economies that rise and fall, cultures that move and shake. We may very well be dealing with the effects of sins committed before we showed up, and those sins' effects may linger, perhaps until after we're gone.

I'll give you some examples of this last point. A friend of mine attends a church in the South that was founded in 1818. He found an old newsletter from the church in which the congregation boasted, "Another thing in our favor is that we have very few negroes in our congregation. They tend to hinder the gospel." Another friend of mine in a congregation on the East Coast found a letter from a former pastor of his church. The letter recounted a deacons' meeting in the 1970s. In that meeting, the deacons discussed integrating their white church in response to the neighborhood becoming more black. One deacon said, "Before we let a nigger join this church, we'll burn this place down."

Given what these churches were boasting about, given how deep the roots of sin are, is it any wonder minorities would be slow to attend them? Is it any wonder these churches have been slow in changing, in blossoming different, diverse fruit? And yet so many of them have changed, by God's grace. The church whose deacons in 1970 were willing to let it burn rather than integrate is now—in God's poetic justice—majority black. My black friend who found those minutes just became its senior pastor! And God, I trust, had a big smile when my friend was installed. Yet these changes took time.

When I mention time and patience in the pursuit of racial progress, I have James Baldwin's words ringing in my ears. He said, "I was born here more than sixty years ago. I'm not going to live another sixty years. You always told me that it's going to take time. It's taken my father's time, my mother's time, my uncle's time, my brother's and my sister's time, my niece's and my nephew's time. How much time do you want for your progress?"[2]

Those are haunting words, aren't they? They remind us that we ought not lazily sit back and presume on God's grace, but rather should do everything we can while it is still day to love our neighbor and care about the weightier matters of the law (Matthew

23:23). And yet we should do so confidently, leaving the results to God. And I know that's easier said than done. I know I'm not alone in wishing I could undo history and injustice and instantly change neighborhoods and churches. But at the end of the day, I cannot.

Pastors, why am I going on about all that we're up against?

I'm going on about it to increase our gratitude. I think that any pastor, after a hard note and departure like José Luis's, would be tempted to scorn the diversity in his congregation or lack thereof. It doesn't feel like that candle is shining particularly bright, does it? But given what we're up against, we should be thankful for whatever diversity we have, however small that flame may be.

I'm going on about it to increase our relief. When you remember how much we're up against, pastors, I hope you remember you can only do so much. And realize that for some people (like José Luis) that still will not be enough—and that's okay. Sometimes, as pastors, we simply have to be content to be misunderstood. More importantly, though, given his racial wounds, José Luis may very well need a different part of Christ's body (i.e., a different local church) to minister to him. And the good news is, he can find it because the kingdom of God is bigger than one individual church. So, as long as José Luis is going to another gospel-preaching church, Pastor Bruce should bless that brother as he goes and thank him for his note. He has pointed out some of Pastor Bruce's blind spots (perhaps more forcefully than he should have), but doing so was a gift to the pastor. At least he knows what José Luis thinks.

Don't Fixate on Making Your Church More Diverse

"But what about the diversity of LRBC?" Pastor Bruce might ask. "What about it?" I'd say. Pastors, we want our churches to look like heaven—people of every tribe and tongue. And that's a wonderful desire; I think the New Testament does encourage churches to be as diverse as they can be. But don't forget that hell is diverse too.[3] We can have a congregation that's diverse and that's poor in love for one another. And what good would that be? In other words, diversity is not the end goal; faithfulness with what God has given us is.

Think of the white church in the middle of nowhere that's surrounded by only white people. Perhaps this community looks the way it does because of an ugly, sinful history (e.g., segregation) that occurred before any of the members or their pastors arrived there (remember my two examples from above). But in the Lord's providence, this is what the community looks like now, and it's not going to change anytime soon. Now let's say this church is committed to praying about racial injustice, and the congregation is more than welcoming to any minority who comes their way, and the preacher boldly addresses matters of ethnicity in his sermons, and they partner with the closest black or Hispanic or Asian church (an hour away) and pray for it regularly. Pastor, I think that white church is glorifying to God. It may not look as impressive, but God sees not as man sees. If we're driven by what *the world* says success regarding race looks like rather than what *the Word* says faithfulness looks like, we'll be crushed, because the world's demands can never be met; that beast is never satisfied.

I say this because I fear that many white pastors make too big a deal about diversity. But diversity can be an idol, one that causes us to look down on churches that are not as diverse as ours. But nowhere does the New Testament prescribe how diverse our churches *must* be. An overemphasis on racial diversity can lead someone to overlook the other types of diversity God has given their congregation (generational, economic, personality type, etc.). While none of these demographics may be as obvious or moving as racial diversity, they are still blessings to steward, cultivate, and praise God for.

Diversity can also be a superficial goal. If we pursue diversity as if our churches should be evenly comprised of all the races of the world, what happens if we actually hit our man-made goal? Do we rest satisfied and stop our work of pursuing lives of justice and mercy? The point isn't for our churches to hit a certain benchmark on a diversity scale. It's for them to be filled with folks who love one another with the love of Christ. This task has no expiration date, nor does it always visibly manifest in spectacular ways. Yet diversity, pursued wrongly, can obsess on *outward* change when what our churches may need is *inward* renewal.

To be sure, diversity can be a powerful testimony to the gospel. But here is the question that should arrest those of us who serve in predominantly white churches: Why is the integration only happening in one direction? That is, why is it that minorities join white churches, but white people by and large do not join churches where they are in the racial minority? Pastor, could it be that what's far more important than getting racial minorities to come to your church is getting your people to go to sound churches where they're in the minority? No, I'm not saying kick out all your white members. But could you challenge them? I remember Mark Dever, senior pastor at Capitol Hill Baptist Church, asking white brothers and sisters in our congregation one Sunday morning, "Are you driving past a faithful black church to come to this church? Why?"

Live a Multiethnic Life

The trend about minorities attending predominantly white churches but not the other way around should push us to remember that if we want a multiethnic church, we must live multiethnic lives. That is, we'll need to regularly spend time with folks of a different ethnicity. If we're unwilling to do this, why would we expect our people to do it? Pastor, if you want a multiethnic church on Sunday, you and your members are going to have to lead multiethnic lives Monday through Saturday.

Pastor Bruce mused about hiring a minority. I think it's great if churches can do so, but I've also seen it go badly. I've seen people place unfair burdens on the brother coming in; I've seen people give up major theological convictions to hire diversely (again, the trouble with idolizing diversity). I've seen churches who *think* they're ready to have a black pastor come, realize they're not—and it's that poor brother and his wife and family who suffer for it the most. We can't expect a hire to be a fix.

A Course of Action

I've gone on long enough about all that Pastor Bruce can't do. Now I'll speak to what he and other pastors can do. There are many questions to consider when it comes to charting a course of action. There's the question of what we might do in our individual capacity as pastors (e.g., one-on-one counseling, private prayer) and our public capacities (e.g., our pulpits). There's the question of the particular needs of our individual congregations: How mature are they? In the wake of a racial tragedy, will I be distracting if I don't say anything? Will I be neglecting different pastoral duties? Pastors, we need much wisdom, so seek out diverse counsel for your particular setting. That said, here's (generally) what we can do:

1. Keep Preaching the Gospel

When the surrounding noise is loud, it's easy to forget to keep preaching the gospel, as basic as that may seem. To be clear, I don't agree with how Brother Mack framed this point in his email to Pastor Bruce—"*I can check the news for politics. I'd encourage you just to keep preaching the gospel rather than steer our church toward overemphasizing one sin the culture is currently fascinated with.*" But remember that who we want to see men and women drawn to is Christ. He is the One we want held high. He draws from every tribe and nation (John 12:32). Keep holding him high. After all, pastors, if we talk about racism more than we talk about Jesus, what are we teaching our people to care about most? But if we keep things of first importance first, we will likely gain a better hearing when we speak on secondary matters. Folks may very well be keener to hear about what we think divides us if our ministries are unflinchingly clear, cheerful, and centered on who unites us—Jesus.

2. Keep Teaching All That Christ Has Commanded

Returning to Brother Mack's "just keep preaching the gospel" line, there's an essentialism there that troubles me. I love the gospel, and I'm a gospel preacher, but we pastors are also to instruct our people on *all that Jesus commanded* (Matthew 28:18–20). We're to instruct them about the weightier matters of the law—justice and mercy. In other words, these matters are matters of discipleship.

I get why Pastor Bruce would be skeptical of some of the books that members of his flock are picking up. The pastor's office does have a preserving nature. In one of his most moving accounts, the apostle Paul told the elders to protect the sheep from false teaching (Acts 20:29–31; cf. Titus 1:9). The sheep could be straying to unhelpful resources, because that's what sheep do—we stray. And so we need to be brought back. But could the sheep also be flocking to unhelpful resources or ideologies because Pastor Bruce hasn't taught as clearly as he should on mercy and justice? Think of Anna Beth and her grievances with the church leadership. As we discussed earlier, Anna Beth has some things to work on, for sure. But is it possible that Pastor Bruce's teaching has not been clear enough to leave members feeling equipped to handle racial matters? I think Anna Beth's critique could easily have been a fair one, namely, that LRBC was more concerned with how not to address racism than with how to address it. Pastors, we have to teach and apply Scripture clearly for our people's sake.

3. Keep Making Space for Differences on Matters That Are Not the Gospel

Pastor, you might have read that last point, about teaching your members positively, and rolled your eyes. *What do you want me to say?* you might think. I understand the sentiment. We may not be experts on race. We don't want to wrongly bind consciences where God has not spoken. And that's just it. I bet you've heard the question a thousand times: "What's our church's position on _____ (fill in the blank: e.g., gentrification)?"

I'd answer that question with another question: "What must every member of this church agree on?" Members of our local congregation must agree on basic tenets of orthodox Christianity (e.g., the Trinity, the physical death and resurrection of Christ, the fallenness of man). We could call these "level 1" issues—things of first importance (1 Corinthians 15:1), what you have to believe to be a Christian. You cannot be a Christian and believe white supremacy or abortion are good, for example. That's tier 1.

Church members must also agree to the basic tenets of our church structure (e.g., leadership structure, baptism). We could call these "level 2" issues—what you have to believe to do church together. An issue being in tier 2 means Christians can disagree on these matters and still be Christians, we just won't be in the same local church. These are the matters that historic Christian denominations disagree over. Both level 1 and level 2 issues are clearly stated in our church's statement of faith, which all members must sign. By so doing, they're saying, "I believe this." On other matters not specified in the first two tiers (e.g., who you should vote for), we allow for differences of opinion and conscience. We could call these "level 3" issues—issues on which there is room for disagreement and Christian freedom. The space for disagreement doesn't mean all opinions are equally valid or true, nor that these opinions shouldn't ever be corrected or challenged. It simply means we won't divide the church over them.[4]

We could see these levels in three concentric circles (see figure).

This philosophy of church unity allows for disagreement on things that are not the gospel or church structure (i.e., levels 1 and 2). But that means this philosophy of unity is necessarily uncomfortable. As Jamie Dunlop observes, "If your church is united around Christ alone, then what is said from the pulpit about important, secondary issues will likely be less forceful, less frequent, and less focused than your convictions would prefer."[5] It's much nicer to go to church with everyone who agrees with you on what you care about. The trouble is, that kind of unity doesn't really say much to the world about the value of Jesus as compared to those other things. Rather, the philosophy of unity outlined above means believers will place different priorities on different issues in level 3, which is to say, you may be in a church with people who think things that you may find repulsive. But this philosophy also allows the church to remain focused on Jesus, rather than on Jesus *and* a particular view of racism, for example. With this view of unity, we may disagree about the merits of this or that philosophy, but neither of us can get excommunicated for our view. And that's the exact opposite of what we see in the larger conversations about race. In the broader conversation, if you don't agree with me, you're out. But in the church, with this view, you're in. We're in this together. And the fact that we choose to remain in this together might very well show the world that though what we are concerned about is important, Jesus is more important. Rather than discourage us, our disagreements can become reminders that we are people who fight to prize Jesus above all.

So, when a church member asks you, "Where does our church stand on _____?" you can say, "We stand together in Christ. We allow for differences of opinion so that you and your sister, whom you disagree with, can both be a part of this church. In other words, the church has no official stance." That's not a cop-out. It's Romans 14. It's living in light of differences. Not everyone agrees with this view of unity. Moreover, currently conversations are being had to highlight whether political positions are becoming level 2 issues, meaning we can only do church with people who share our political sympathies. But I believe that if Jesus can bring Jew and Gentile together, surely he can bring people from different political parties together.

4. Keep Being Willing to Ruffle Feathers

Just because we allow for differences on level 3 does not mean we don't teach basic principles or call people to repentance. Remember how Pastor Bruce thought Brother Mack didn't intend to be racially partial, and that he still considered him a good brother? But regardless of Brother Mack's *intentions*, he was still having a negative *impact* on those around him—impact we as pastors wouldn't want. And so, pastor, we must teach and apply Scripture. Of course this teaching will ruffle some feathers. What sinner doesn't have his feathers ruffled now and then? But be sure not to conflate "ruffled feathers" with "disunity."

I spoke about the dangers of idolizing diversity above, but we can also idolize unity. That is, we'll do anything (or not do or say some things) to preserve the peace. But to do that can be tantamount to declaring, "Peace, peace," when there is no peace. Martin Luther King Jr. spoke about this in his "Letter from a Birmingham Jail," speaking to the "white moderate, who is more devoted to 'order' than to justice; who prefers a negative peace which is the absence of tension to a positive peace which is the presence of justice."[6] I fear that, out of a desire for comfort, too many evangelicals have relegated matters of race to the "political realm" or "social realm," not realizing that R. L. Dabney—a full-throated, slavery-defending Southern Presbyterian—did the same. Hence, they've divorced these matters from the discipling of their members.

5. Keep Praying

The need to continue praying is obvious, but I fear that prayer has been denigrated as we think about how to pursue racial justice. Pastor, keep praying, privately and publicly. One type of prayer that I'd highlight is the practice of lament. For what it's worth, I think it was good for Pastor Bruce to have Darius share that word of hope, though I hope he won't leave Darius to do all the sharing in moments of racial upheaval. As a racial minority, it's powerful and refreshing to hear someone from the majority speak to the issues. That said, I hope our churches are places where it is okay to be sad. In other words, before we rush to hope, let's make sure we sit in the sadness. Our God will sit there with us. He is near to the brokenhearted. And so we grieve freely. We lament deeply. American churches, frankly, are bad at this. We like triumph! Conquering! Hoo-rah!

On this point of lament, I think Brother Mack is both wrong and right. He's wrong in that he thinks lament is inappropriate in the public gathering, or that we should only do it when a victim's name has been cleared. We can still generally lament a tragedy. Jesus lamented Lazarus's death, even though he knew he was going to raise him. Paul said, "Weep with those who weep" (Romans 12:15), not "Weep with those who weep *in so far as you agree with the reason for their weeping or share their moral sympathies.*" Brother Mack told Pastor Bruce that the church should lament more issues, like abortion. I think he's right. We should lament abortion, and many evangelical churches do. But there are no limits to the issues we can lament. The problem of churches in America seems to be not that we lament too much, but that we lament far too little.

This point of lament raises a sad and sweet memory for me. One Sunday evening in 2015, my wife, who is white, and I were walking to our church in Washington, DC. A white man walking past us started loudly singing, "Too many niggers! Too many niggers!" When I turned around in anger, he said, "What? Rape is the number one problem in DC, and you're surprised, nigger?" During all of this, I hadn't noticed, but two white church members were walking behind us and heard the whole exchange. The following Sunday, one of the pastors had me share this encounter with the congregation. We wept—together.

When someone asks what the church is "going to do" on racial matters, the pastor's answer could be very simple: "We're going to pray a lot and lament a lot and talk a lot."[7]

6. Keep Talking and Keep Having Your People Share Their Stories

Stories do something to us. They're powerful, especially when they're from people we know and love. Reading an excerpt from a historic, primary source is one thing, mighty as it may be. But, man, having that elderly saint whom the church adores talk about segregation in front of the whole church—that can be quite another thing. Pastors, we should be having these conversations out of season as well as in season—that is, not just when a racial tragedy strikes. I know one white brother whose church was having weekend conferences about race when nothing "major" was going on about race in the news. So, when the news like that of Malachi Brewers broke, they were ready—not because the news wasn't a big deal to them, but precisely the opposite: it *was* a big deal because they had already been regularly thinking, speaking, and praying about race.

Teach and Teach Some More

The suggestions I've listed for Pastor Bruce are not revolutionary. Most of them center around teaching. Pastors, there's much we could do—and no doubt, some of the sheep in our congregations want their pastors to be more than pastors (and their churches to be more than churches). But a pastor is primarily a *teacher*. And teaching is powerful! It shapes people who scatter into the world to do good works. So teach and teach some more.

If you're a pastor, you'll get difficult emails like the ones Pastor Bruce received. But God is going to keep us. Let's remember a lot of believers have gone before us in much more difficult circumstances. We have not yet resisted to the point of shedding our blood.

Questions for Reflection and Discussion

1. How have you treated your pastor as he navigates racial tensions? Have you reached out to him to talk about race matters? Have you encouraged him? Criticized him? Why or why not?

2. When it comes to matters of race and racism, how does realizing more of what we're up against change our perspective?

3. What are some pitfalls of idolizing unity? Of idolizing diversity?

4. Take some time to pray for your pastor now.

PART

2

If anyone thinks he is religious and does not bridle his tongue . . . this person's religion is worthless.

—JAMES 1:26

Refrain from violence of fist, tongue, or heart.

—COMMANDMENT 8 OF MARTIN LUTHER KING JR.'S PLEDGE FOR VOLUNTEERS[1]

CHAPTER 7

WHY SHOULD WE TALK ABOUT RACE ACROSS COLOR LINES?

Is Christ divided?

—1 CORINTHIANS 1:13

The local church should reflect the truth about God. If it is divided, it teaches everyone that Christ is divided. If love does not mark your church, then it may attract spiritual hobbyists . . . who like to play at religion, but not people of real Christian love who will inconvenience themselves for others.

—MARK DEVER[1]

A s we begin this workbook's second half, we break from our story for three chapters. That may be frustrating, but I don't want us to rush to the end of our story without clearly answering some important questions that pertain to our lives. After all, it's real life we're talking about here. We're not hypothesizing about fictional characters for mere intrigue. We're talking about matters that affect real flesh and blood. Real churches. Real divisions. Real hopelessness. Real grief. I feel that grief even now. As I write this chapter, the US Capitol, which sits five blocks from my home in Washington, DC, is in lockdown.

A group of protesters have violently stormed the Capitol in attempts to "Stop the Steal!" (That is, the protesters are seeking to invalidate what they understand to be a fraudulent presidential election.) I see a protester brazenly waving the Confederate flag in the Capitol. I think about how much this insurrection encapsulates the racial division and animosity of the present day. I feel disoriented and yet unsurprised this sixth day of January 2021. And I feel the weight of these three questions even more:

1. Why should we talk about race across color lines? (chapter 7)
2. Why is it so hard to talk about race across color lines? (chapter 8)
3. How should we talk about race across color lines? (chapter 9)

Our fictional friends have shown us something of the answers. But like life itself, their display has been messy. Inconsistent. Mixed. A look at things unjumbled will lend helpful clarity as we see not only how our characters should speak across color lines, but also how we should speak. And yet that's our first question: *Should we speak?*

If you're anything like me, you're not always sure. Given how hard it can be to talk about race across color lines, we might often wonder, *Why bother?* Why waste time and energy talking to *them*, whoever "them" might be? After all, not all hard conversations are worth having. In fact, there is a category of foolish controversy the Lord's servants should avoid, and some conversations about race are not exempt (2 Timothy 2:14, 24–26; Titus 3:1–2). But does this mean we should avoid all or even most conversations about race across color lines? Judging by how we Christians can shy away from one another on these matters, it seems we think so. But what's at stake if we don't speak to one another? That's what we'll think about in this chapter.

The General Answer: Love

Why bother? In response to this question, we could offer a simple and biblical answer: love. *Christians should bother to talk about race across color lines because love compels us.*

Love for God. Love for sharing the good news about him. Love for our neighbor. This isn't a controversial point, right? *Christians love*—or at least we should. The trouble is, when it comes to talking about race across color lines, we sometimes disagree on the best way to express that love. Indeed, some Christians avoid cross-color conversations about these matters not *despite* their love for others but *because* of it.

Some Christians legitimately see cross-color conversations as a distraction from the more important and neglected work of loving the oppressed. Other Christians cite personal experiences that make them reasonably certain these conversations are futile. Some Christians understand these conversations to make race a problem when there is no problem. And, as we'll soon see, there are times when the best thing not only for ourselves but for the person we're talking to is to stop a conversation. Reasons exist, good and bad, why Christians avoid these conversations out of love. But generally, I maintain that love, as Scripture defines it, should push us into, not away from, these conversations. Why?

The Specific Answer(s)

Here are six reasons we should engage in conversations about race across color lines.

1. Out of Love for Our God and for His Glory

Yes, conversations about race can be hard, but hard doesn't necessarily mean bad. So often when conversations about race come up, they're framed negatively—and we've seen why. But aren't these conversations more fundamentally wonderful stages for God's glory? When we speak up for those who cannot speak for themselves, *God is glorified* (Proverbs 31:8). When we bear with and forgive one another, *God is glorified* (Colossians 3:13). It is through the church—specifically Jew and Gentile being made into one new man through Christ—that God is making his manifold wisdom known, Ephesians 3:10 says. And in so far as our conversations about race help us to maintain and display that blood-bought unity, *God is glorified*.

As Christians, we don't seek to be glory thieves but glory givers in all things. So if we're truly living to please God, whether we're eating, drinking, or talking about race, we should do it all for God's glory. And it is his glory, friends, that will motivate us to keep enduring in these discussions.

If we talk about race because it's trendy, we won't last when the trials come. We'll be driven and tossed by the wind. But if we talk about race because we believe it matters for the glory of God, we will press on despite challenge or blessing, slander or praise, resistance or repentance. Of course we can take breaks from the conversation. This isn't the only conversation to have. But as long as we have a God to glorify, we have a conversation to take up toward that end. Let all we speak about race be because we love God first and foremost. Loving God with our all is the first and greatest commandment.

2. Out of Love for Our Neighbors and for Their Relief

The second commandment is like the first: to love those who bear God's image. Conversations about race can educate us on ways we can better love our neighbors. In this sense, these conversations offer yet another way for us to "stir up one another to love and good works" as Hebrews 10:24 speaks about. I raise this point because in conversations about race, it's easy for us to get distracted.

Think of the parable of the good Samaritan, in which the religious folks walk past the broken man. Now, imagine if the religious intended to stop and help the man, but first they argued with each other about why the man needed help. The priest says, "Well, I think his suffering is his fault," and the Levite responds, "Well, I think it was the system that beat him down," and back and forth they go. And all the while the broken man says, "Hey guys, I'm still over here, bleeding." Though we may be having fruitful debate about a matter or three with someone, we should realize that while we're debating, our neighbor still might very well be on the side of the road, bleeding.

In other words, our neighbors are not mere conversation points. They're people to love. You might think a local, impoverished community looks the way it does for one reason, and a fellow church member might think it looks that way for a different reason. But if you both could agree that it needs help, could you find a common solution and work to implement it, as Samantha Lee and Anna Beth did for Anna Beth's classroom? The answer is yes—unless you both spend most of your time arguing with one another. Racial discussions shouldn't become distractions from helping our neighbors. They should be means for us to learn how to better love them. We could ask the following three questions about any given issue to produce more fruitful, specific conversation about racial issues:

1. The historical question: What happened?
2. The judicial question: Was it right?
3. The ethical question: What should we do about it, if anything?

3. Out of Love for Our Brothers and Sisters, and for Their Holiness

At the church where I serve as a pastor, we have a covenant that every member signs upon joining the church. It's essentially a set of promises we make to one another for how we'll live with one another as members of the church. One line of that covenant says, "We will walk together in brotherly love . . . exercise an affectionate care and watchfulness over each other and faithfully admonish and entreat one another as occasion may require." There's nothing unique about this aspect of our covenant. It reflects something that Christians do: we point out blind spots and sin to one another. The topic of race isn't exempt from this duty.

Now, with that said, sometimes on the topic of race we can be zealous—really zealous—to point out blind spots. And if we're not careful, our zeal won't just be off-putting or uncharitable, bad as those things are, but it will also be "demonic," as James wrote (James 3:13–18).

Friends, here's a simple test to know whether our zeal in confronting racial blind spots is from Satan or from God. When considering your zeal, answer these three questions:

1. Does it have more wrath than love?
2. Does it disgrace your brother more than cure him?
3. Does it divide more than heal?

If the answer to any of these questions is yes, your zeal is from Satan.[2] As you consider admonishing your brothers and sisters about race, here are a few more questions to ask yourself:

Do I need to give this brother or sister this admonishment, or can our relationship continue unaffected if I don't? If you do decide to give the admonishment, ask yourself:

Do I need to give this brother or sister this admonishment *right now*? Is this moment or this platform the best space to do so? Proverbs 25:11 says, "Like apples of gold in settings of silver is a word spoken in right circumstances" (NASB). If you decide that now is indeed the best time for the admonishment, finally, ask yourself this:

Do I hug this person harder than I hit them? Of course I don't mean physically. But do you encourage those people you disagree with for the good they're doing or the good points they're making *more* than you criticize them? Beloved, a general rule of thumb is that hugging is more powerful than hitting. Hugging heals; hitting divides. And divisions matter.

4. Out of Love for Our Unity and for Its Testimony

It's tempting to think, *Maybe I should just go to church where everyone agrees with me on racial issues.* But keep in mind that more is at stake than your comfort. That's not to say you shouldn't ever leave your church over these matters, as we saw with Darius, but rather that you should give sticking with your church your best shot. Why? Because there is a corporate testimony, an evangelistic witness at stake.

Jesus said in John 13:35 that the world will know we are his disciples by how we love one another. Jesus prayed in John 17:21 that Christians would be one so the world would believe the Father had sent him. God be praised, Jesus didn't leave that unity up to us. He went ahead and secured it in his blood. Through the cross, Ephesians 2:11–22 says that God has made one new humanity. Through the cross, God has reconciled those who turn from their sins and trust in Jesus both to God and to one another.

When it comes to racial strife between Christians, our union with one another isn't affected, but our communion—our fellowship—is. And the world can tell. Francis Schaeffer commented on John 17:21, "Upon his authority [Jesus] gives the world the right to judge whether you and I are born-again Christians, on the basis of our observable love toward all Christians. . . . The world may not understand what the Christians are disagreeing about, but they will very quickly understand the difference of our differences . . . if they see us having our differences in an open and observable love on a practical level."[3]

When it comes to race, history speaks loudly about American evangelical churches' failure to maintain the unity of the Spirit in the bond of peace, and this is to our shame. We had both the obligation and the opportunity to shine as a light to the world. Consider how striking it would have been for a white, fundamentalist church member in the 1950s to say, "Hey, world! This man who has darker skin—who you say is unworthy—he is my brother and my equal in every way, and he is welcome to our Lord's table. He is welcome to have full membership privileges within this church right alongside me. And if you have a problem with him, you have a problem with me, because we are united in the Lord Jesus Christ!" And yet too many white parishioners throughout American history did the exact opposite. They didn't oppose racial injustice. They gave it moral and spiritual sanction, compounding and perpetuating it.[4]

We could summarize the need to keep talking about racial matters in one sentence: *We should talk about racial matters because of the American evangelical church's disturbing track record on race relations.* We should talk about them because, in so far as our ability to talk about them is broken, our fellowship will be too. We should talk about them because, in so far as Christians cannot have honest conversations about these matters, our fellowship will be both a sham and a scandal to a watching world. If we care about evangelism, we should care about racism too.

I recognize this is a hard word, but I've said it because I believe that by God's grace we can do better. I believe we still have an opportunity to stun the world with our love for one another, and I pray that we all are asking, "How can Christians love each other today on matters of race in such a way that the world has no choice but to say, 'Wow! Look at how those Christians love one another!'"

As history shows, such love will not come without opposition. Earlier we talked about pressing into these matters for God's glory. One primary way our unity glorifies God is by bearing witness to God. And Satan hates that witness. One reason the race conversation is so hard is because we are not wrestling against flesh and blood. Ever since the church started, Acts 6:1–7 shows us, Satan has loved to quake the church along ethnic and cultural fault lines. Why has he enjoyed shaking God's people in such a way? Because doing so keeps people from seeing Jesus.[5]

5. Out of Love for Our Doctrine and Its Soundness

Faithful conversations about race—those had in light of God's Word—can help guard against the promotion of falsehoods. And if we turn a blind eye to them, those falsehoods can run. Now, to be sure, we can disagree on what the truth of a matter is, and that presents its own difficulty. But there are some facts we need to be clear on that evangelical churches haven't always been clear on—or, even worse, they have been clear on these issues in the wrong ways. Take interracial marriage, for example. Some Christians might say that God opposes it. *No, he does not.*

We talked about unity in our last point. Yet if we don't have the conversations we need to have, disunity will result. And you know what? If we're not careful, so will unsound doctrine.

Therefore, we need to talk to one another. And we ought not to be the overbearing heresy patrol, going around policing every conversation. *"You said this one idea in which I find a whiff of ideological impurity—wham!—you're out."* Remember, hugging not hitting. But with that reminder, let's talk. In doing so, we help one another guard the truth. Every Christian has a vested interest in guarding the truth according to Galatians 1 and Ephesians 4. And if the truth is protected, the hope of the gospel can be held out to a dying world.

6. Out of Love for Sinners and for Their Hope

If we don't talk about race matters, we will confuse people about what the sin of racism is and obscure the hope there is in Christ in regard to it—a hope people need now as much as ever.

Consider for a moment that brother or sister for whom "racist" is the worst thing they could be called. Now, maybe they'd react so poorly to the charge because it's unfair or untrue. But perhaps they'd react poorly to it because they have skirted race issues for so long that they are unprepared for how to deal with them when confronted. Could it be they've just been left to define these matters on their own? Maybe they already have a definition of *racist* or *prejudiced*, and in their mind, they're not it.

But even Christians can harbor prejudices. It is possible for us to be complicit in systems that promote ethnic partiality. I'm not as interested in whether prejudices and complicity make one a "racist" as I am in our honesty with ourselves. Do we really want to say it's not possible for us to harbor prejudices or be complicit in larger systems? The psalmist knew he had hidden faults (Psalm 19:12). What about you?

Going back to why this conversation is so hard, it's hard because some of us may have prejudices we don't even realize we have. Have you ever had an ethnically prejudiced thought in your life—in your Christian life? I have.

But there's good news. The scandal of the gospel isn't that

Christians can commit racism; the scandal of the gospel is that Christ forgives those who repent of the sin of racism. And to eschew talking about race is to hold back that great hope. In a striking comment, James Baldwin said that racism devours both its victim *and its perpetrator.*[6] We should have pity on anyone who shows ethnic partiality. We should hold out hope to them, for they might not have it otherwise.

The world defends or denies sin. *Christians* confess sin because he who is faithful and just to forgive our sins will cleanse us from all unrighteousness (1 John 1:9). So let's not act like racism is the sin that can't ever be committed, and let's not act like it's a sin that can't ever be forgiven. Talking about these matters can help us not act that way.

A Time to Speak

When we talk about racial issues, we have the opportunity to be ministers of hope. We've talked about hope for those who commit racism, but what about those who receive it? Is it any wonder why someone might think Christianity is a white man's religion if we act as if it has nothing to say to them? Oh, but it does! Fannie Lou Hamer knew so.

A Christian woman whose trust in the Lord was as sturdy as her voice was beautiful, Mrs. Hamer would be known as the lady "who know how to sing." Belting traditional spirituals as she helped bring about voting rights in the early 1960s, Mrs. Hamer was traveling in Mississippi when she was kicked out of a transportation facility. The Interstate Commerce Commission had legally mandated this transportation facility to be integrated, so she, as a black woman, had every right to be there. The people who kicked her out were white police officers. They took her to a jail—supposedly to interrogate her. Tragically, they were more interested in beating her than in hearing her answers to their questions. And yet Mrs. Hamer, committed to nonviolence, resolved to love those men—and all white men and women. A simple gospel woman with profound impact, she'd later say, "Ain't no such thing as I can hate anybody and hope to see God's face."

Mrs. Hamer would soon meet the wife of one of the jailers, a white woman who gave her some water. Mrs. Hamer thanked her and remarked that she "must be Christian people." Charles Marsh tells the story:

> The jailer's wife picked up on Mrs. Hamer's remark, telling her that she really tried her best to live right and to please God. Mrs. Hamer assumed the role of counselor and told the jailer's wife to get out her Bible and read Proverbs 26:26 and Acts 17:26.
>
> Though his hatred be covered with deception,
>> his wickedness will be exposed in the assembly. (Proverbs 26:26)
>
> [God] made from one man every nation of mankind to live on all the face of the earth, having determined allotted periods and the boundaries of their dwelling place. (Acts 17:26)
>
> Mrs. Hamer's counsel, spoken in the spirt of gentleness and edification, offered at the same time an effective one-two punch of divine judgment and costly forgiveness. There is nothing sanguine about reconciliation in these passages.[7]

God has spoken about these matters, and so we speak. Imperfectly, yes—no one is perfect in what they say (James 3:2). But we speak sincerely. We speak faithfully. We don't have to choose between having conversations and pursuing justice. We can have conversations as a part of our pursuit of justice. Would that we do so, especially when the conversations get tough. And it's to that issue, the difficulty of the conversation, we now turn.

Questions for Reflection and Discussion

1. Which of the six reasons for engaging in conversations about race across color lines resonated with you the most? Why?
2. Which reason did you disagree with most, if any? Why?
3. How does the gospel uniquely give hope to both perpetrators and victims of racism? Does the gospel give you hope regarding racism? Why or why not?
4. Before moving on to the next part of this workbook, pray that you would be more honest, hopeful, and humble in conversations about race.

CHAPTER 8

WHY IS IT SO HARD TO TALK ABOUT RACE ACROSS COLOR LINES?

What causes quarrels and what causes fights among you? Is it not this, that your passions are at war within you?

—JAMES 4:1

While we write and print millions of words about race in America, why is it still so hard to have a truly respectful, decent, and humble dialogue about perhaps the most complicated and contentious issue in American life?

—DAVID FRENCH[1]

Here is something anyone building anything from IKEA has learned: language matters. Why IKEA cannot simply write out their instructions alongside their pictures, I do not know. But I do know that communication is essential for progress—just ask the builders of the Tower of Babel. How often do our conversations about race feel like we're building there—in that land of division and strife? Unlike the builders at Babel, however, we're not trying to build something for our glory. We're striving to build up our churches for God's glory. We're striving to love our brothers, sisters, and neighbors. Yet the same, simple principle remains: if we want to make progress regarding race, we must be able to speak with each other. Why can't we do that?

An Equally Obvious and Important Question

Before we answer the question, let's briefly meditate on the power of words. After all, it may seem like a waste of time to talk about, well, talking. Yet the question, "Why is it so hard to talk about race?" is as obvious as it is important. The trouble is, we often assume or speed past the obvious things, don't we? When it comes to race, there are other good things we want—justice, unity, and so forth. But what if we could better pursue these ends if we thought a bit more about the obvious? What if thinking deeper would help us travel further together?

Friend, we're speaking about speaking because words are important. Words are a big part of what distinguishes the one true God from the fake gods. The living God speaks (Habakkuk 2:18–19)! With words God created and upholds a universe, and with words Satan tricked our first parents into spoiling it. Just read how much Romans 3 says about speech. Consider Jesus saying that he'll judge all our words (Matthew 12:36). We've all learned, likely the hard way, that the motto "sticks and stones may break my bones, but words can never hurt me!" is a lie. Indeed, "death and life are in the power of the tongue" (Proverbs 18:21). We can't overestimate the importance of thinking about our speech.

Think for a moment about how different race relations would be today if white churches during the period of Reconstruction and Jim Crow would have excommunicated unrepentant segregationists within their congregations. Consider how different the racial makeup of churches would look today if churches would have simply *declared the truth* about racial equality instead of perpetuating the lie of racial hierarchy. Speaking the truth matters more than we realize. So, why is it so hard to do that when it comes to race?

The General Answer: Sin

On one level, we could simply say *sin*. That's our foundational answer, and it's a wise one. This is James's answer: "What causes quarrels and what causes fights among you? Is it not this, that your passions are at war within you?" (4:1).

James essentially said, "You got a beef? It's because you got sin." And even if it's not our sin, the curse of sin—the frustration of this fallen order that causes us to groan, as Romans 8:22–23 talks about—troubles our conversations.

So sin is the reason it's so hard to talk about race. But that's an unsatisfying answer, isn't it? You likely already knew these conversations are hard because of sin. But even more than that, "sin" doesn't exactly answer our question about why *race*—as opposed to other topics—is so hard for Christians to talk about. After all, Christians talk about lots of things in this fallen world with far less difficulty than we do race: work, sports, prayer, parenting. I'm not saying those conversations are always easy, but not many of them get us going quite like race. So, what gives?

James's epistle helps us here. Notice it doesn't stop at James 4:1. James goes on to name specific sins—what they are and who generally commits them—alongside other pastoral concerns. For instance, in James 5:1–4, James explicitly warns the rich of God's coming judgment for their sin of defrauding poor field workers. This passage sounds a lot like Proverbs 13:23, "An unplowed field produces food for the poor, but injustice sweeps it away" (NIV). So we can see that while "sin" was James's answer to the question about why Christians are in conflict, it was not his only answer. He dove deeper.

The Specific Answer(s)

We're going to follow James's lead. We've presented the general answer. Now we'll dive deeper into "sin" and other issues so we can make progress. In what follows, we're going to break out specific reasons why talking about race is so hard. Here's how we'll do that. We're going to look at bad fruit—that is, the things we evidently see happening in our conversations, and then we're going to look at the root of that fruit—that is, the reason it's happening. The fruit is the *what*. The root is the *why*.

Why Is It So Hard for Christians of Different Stripes to Talk about Race with Each Other?

Fruits and Roots

Fruit 1: We try to have every conversation in every conversation because . . .

Root 1: Race and racism are broad topics.

I often call race the "Velcro issue" because so many aspects of life stick to it: politics, housing, economics, education, or other aspects of life. I remember my mother sharing about the first time she had a chili dog. She was five years old and living in Fayetteville, North Carolina. She ate at a segregated lunch counter and was not allowed to use the restroom because she was black. Racism had reached the bathroom, the kitchen counter, a little girl's plate, and her memory too. Given the vastness of the topic of race, oftentimes our conversations about it are hard because we don't know where to begin, and we certainly don't have the competency to speak to every topic.

What Can We Do? Specify.

We can try to locate our real disagreements. Kevin DeYoung speaks to why doing so proves helpful.

> With racial matters, we are often guilty of making every conversation about everything else. So even though the disagreement started off by talking about colonial American history, we ended up arguing about Donald Trump, mass incarceration, and corporate repentance. To be sure, sometimes everything is connected to everything, but I still maintain that our conversations will produce more light than heat if we can focus in on one argument at a time. . . . By more carefully isolating our real disagreements, we will be better equipped to talk responsibly, listen respectfully, find common ground, and move in the direction of possible solutions.[2]

If we're going to make progress, we're going to have to move beyond vague agreements that racism is bad and reconciliation is good. Specific conversations—in which we share specific hopes, specific fears, specific dreams—can help us do that.

Fruit 2: We don't always agree on what the injustice of racism is because . . .

Root 2: Race and racism are complex topics.

Consider the idea of *race* for a moment. When it comes to race, what exactly are we talking about—a reality? A fiction? A biological fiction but a social fact? How many races are there? Has the answer changed over time, and how? And what does Scripture say about these questions? Have Christians always shared an understanding of what it says?

Now consider *racism*. Christians agree that racism is sin.

But what that sin particularly is—how clearly it manifests, the extent to which it runs throughout society, and who perpetuates it—that's a different story, isn't it? You might have read what I said above about the Velcro nature of racism and disagreed! What's more, when it comes to race and racism, we're not just dealing with sin. We're dealing with ideas and cultures that have molded and morphed over time. We're dealing with the implications of other convictions we hold. For instance, take the mission of the church—what we believe the church's mission to be will impact how we think the church should respond to racism. And that's just one example. We could keep listing examples, but it's clear that often our conversations about race are hard because the topics are complicated.

And perhaps this complexity explains one reason we quarrel so much about race. After all, arguing is easier than coming up with solutions to complex problems. Implementing solutions, on the other hand, takes thought, wisdom, creativity, and endurance. It's much easier to burn a house down than build one. It's much easier to criticize than create. And given the complexities of the present racial problems, many of us, if we're honest, prefer the easy route.

What Can We Do? Study.

We can study. We can read. We can learn. In listing all those questions about race and racism earlier in this point, my goal wasn't to confuse you but to show you the difficulty of the matters at hand. Yet the plethora of questions or lack of agreement on the answers doesn't mean the disputes about race are unimportant. It doesn't mean the questions don't have true answers that can be taught, learned, and clarified. It doesn't mean we should just "agree to disagree" on all these important discussions. Rather, the abundance of questions and rebuttals means that the answers will take work. Bible-open, like the Bereans in Acts 17:11, Scripture-examining work. In chapter 11 you can find my list of suggested books to begin with on race.

Fruit 3: Sometimes we speak harshly because . . .

Root 3: Race and racism are painful topics.

It's one thing for a subject to be complicated. Take the Trinity, for instance. It's complex. It's a mystery. And though it is one that deeply—more than anything—bears upon our existence, it is not an issue spoken about with half as much angst as race. No doubt, the early church had its painful controversies over the Trinity. While those controversies are still relevant, the pain of them is largely removed from our context today. After all, no people group in recent memory has been enslaved because of their view of the Trinity. At least in the history of America, no civil wars have been incited over beliefs about God's triune nature. No one was redlined by the Federal Housing Administration for being a Unitarian.

But when it comes to race, we're dealing with matters many people understand to touch upon the core of their identity, so the matters are personal. When it comes to race, we're dealing with matters people see in the faces of their children, and so the matters are cherished. When it comes to race, we're dealing with matters many people understand to have financially picked their pockets, so the matters are costly. When it comes to race, we're dealing with matters many Christians understand themselves to suffer from today, and so the matters are relevant. When it comes to race, we're dealing with matters that stir up raw memories of rejection and indignity and violence, so the matters are tender. They're painful.

And because racial issues are so painful, they make our conversations weighty and hard, and sometimes those of us who are in pain speak out of that pain. We lash out. We exaggerate. We're acerbic. Maybe it's because we feel we won't be heard otherwise. Or maybe it's simply because hurt people tend to hurt people.

What Can We Do? Remember and Forgive.

Remember that it's possible to be angry but not sin (Psalm 4:4; Ephesians 4:26). In other words, sometimes it's okay to be angry. Sometimes it's right. Remember, however, that revenge belongs to God (Romans 12:19). And remember that he didn't take vengeance out on you when he would have been right to do so. Reflecting on God's mercy, Esau McCaulley shares a lesson all Christians can learn from black Christians who are righteously angry over racism: "The profound act of [God's] mercy gives us the theological resources to forgive. What do Black Christians do with the rage that we rightly feel? We send it to the cross of Christ."[3]

Fruit 4: Sometimes we don't give the conversation enough weight because . . .

Root 4: Race and racism aren't painful topics for everyone.

One reason conversations about race are so hard is because we come to the table with vastly different experiences. So someone may be talking about race, but in a detached manner. For this person, racism is engaged as an idea and not an experience. And what do we do with ideas? We evaluate them. We test them. We think about them in the abstract, poking and prodding to evaluate the truthfulness of claims against what we previously understood to be true. This may be fine in some sense, if the folks we're talking to likewise know racism as an idea rather than an experience.

However, when speaking with someone who has been on the receiving end of racism, speaking in such a theoretical manner can be unhelpful. It not only grieves your listener, but it also frustrates the conversation. As we've just considered, when many folks think of racism, they're not thinking in abstractions. They're thinking about things that have happened to them and those they love. For them, racism isn't a mental exercise or a matter of talking points. It's an experience they didn't have the luxury of dodging.[4]

What Can We Do? Localize Our Experience.

Frankly, the temptation to speak about race abstractly is a greater temptation for my white brothers and sisters.[5] One simple thing you can do is be aware of what we've just described. Don't universalize your experience. Rather, recognize that someone else may have a real and very different experience, one that you should appreciate as worthy of great sorrow.

Fruit 5: We disagree on how to apply the Bible to issues of race because . . .

Root 5: We read the Bible in different ways.

"Both read the same Bible and pray to the same God and each invokes His aid against the other."[6] Abraham Lincoln said this in his second inaugural address to a war-torn country. And it seems, while to a lesser degree, the same problem remains. The problem isn't the Bible; it's that we have different notions of how to apply the Bible. A friend of mine put it deftly: "One reason believers disagree on issues like systemic racism is that we have different intuitions about common grace insights. Some hold deep suspicion (whether consciously or not) about secular scholarship; others are more open to it as an expression of common

grace. So, Christians who agree on paper about the suffi-
ciency of Scripture still end up with different instincts about
how to apply Scripture to the ethical challenges of our day."[7]

What Can We Do? Name This Difference.

Scripture is clear in its basic teaching about the gospel.
Moreover, no one is allowed to read the Bible however they
want. That said, simply recognizing that there can be legitimate differences in how Christians draw implications from
Scripture can go a long way toward engendering charity in
hard conversations.

Fruit 6: We don't know how to talk to one another because . . .

Root 6: Our churches are (largely) racially segregated.

Perhaps we could recognize the differences in how
we approach Scripture if we knew one another. But many
American neighborhoods are segregated, and so are their
churches. Space forbids discussing whether this segregation
is de facto, de jure, or some mix of the two—but the point
is, despite the rise in interracial evangelical churches, most
are divided.[8] And it cannot be denied that this segregation is
because of racism in the past. As historian Jemar Tisby notes,
"There would be no black church without racism in the
white church."[9]

One distressing effect of this segregation is that it's hard
to get to know one another. And so we may very well be
ignorant of how members of another ethnicity operate or
speak, or of what they've gone through. And often we fill
the void of our knowledge with false assumptions and narratives that frustrate any potential conversations further still.

What Can We Do? Build Relationships with People Not like Us.

The trend toward multiethnic evangelical churches is that minorities attend predominantly white churches, not vice versa.[10] Until we see the trend going in both directions, where whites will attend faithful gospel churches where they are not in the racial majority, conversations about race will continue to be difficult.[11]

Fruit 7: We fight and quarrel on social media because . . .

Root 7: We're having "conversations" in the wrong place.

While great good can be accomplished through social media, it, by definition, inhibits many aspects of conversation (e.g., tone, body language). It discourages other aspects of helpful conversation (e.g., nuance). It rewards inattention—the faster you scroll, the more content you get. It rewards haughtiness; the more polemical you are, the more likes you get. And we've not yet discussed the sad reality that some of us listen to bloggers or tweeters *more* than to the pastors God has placed over us.

While these challenges may not be unique to online conversations about race as opposed to other topics, social media has contributed something unique to the racial discourse in America: a horrifying genre of videos of black image bearers being killed.

Think back to the last racial tragedy you witnessed. How did you learn about it? Was it through social media? Think back to the place you saw people squabbling about it. Was it on social media? Am I saying get off Twitter, Facebook, and the rest? No. But I am saying to be careful with them. After all, social media has a disinhibition effect, where it emboldens us to say words online that we would never say in person.

What Can We Do? Talk Face-to-Face.

How much better would conversations about race be if we had them across our dinner tables rather than across the internet? This point connects to our last. If we're segregated, we can't talk face-to-face. And even if we have racially integrated networks and churches, are we taking advantage of them? How many people in your church have never stepped foot, much less had a meal in the home of someone of a different ethnicity? Though social media didn't exist in his day, and though he had much to say, John recognized that some conversations were better "face to face" (3 John 13–14). And we need to recognize the same when it comes to speaking of race.

Fruit 8: We don't know what to say at times because . . .

Root 8: We're conflicted and lack wisdom.

One reason that conversations about race are so hard is because when they come up, we can easily be conflicted or realize just how weak our words are. Moreover, in racial conversations, as in any conversation, there is a time to answer fools and a time not to—and it's not always clear which time is which (Proverbs 26:4–5).

What Can We Do? Discern Whether It Is a Time to Speak or a Time to Be Silent.

When conflicted, here are a few questions to ask to determine whether you should continue a conversation about race.

- **Have I prayed about speaking with this person?** If you lack wisdom as to whether you should talk to that person, do what Scripture says: ask God (James 1:5). When Paul wanted love to abound, what did he do? He asked God (Philippians 1:9; 1 Thessalonians 3:12).

- **Do I have a responsibility to say something?** Is this a situation in which I should be a voice for the voiceless (Proverbs 31:8–9) or point out a brother's or sister's sin (Matthew 18:15–20; Galatians 6:1)? Or am I grabbing a dog by its ears—entering a quarrel not my own, one I shouldn't enter (Proverbs 3:30; 26:17)?

- **Is this conversation good for my heart or my listener's heart (Proverbs 4:23)?** By beginning or continuing this conversation, am I signing up for unnecessary discouragement? Am I needlessly repeating an offense (Proverbs 17:9)?

- **Is this conversation good for the building up of my church (1 Corinthians 14:26)?** Will this conversation result in the building up or the tearing down of my church? If brothers and sisters were to listen in on this conversation, would they be challenged and helped or disheartened and grieved?

- **Is this person I'm talking to given to unrighteous anger or division (Proverbs 22:24; Romans 16:17)?** Scripture is clear: we should avoid these kinds of people.

- **Is this person interested in a good-faith conversation (Proverbs 9:8)?** Do they want to make friends or make a point? Do they want to win over people or win an argument? Are they willing to be won? In other words, are they open to their mind being changed? If not, consider talking with people who actually want to have a conversation. There are lots of them out there, and you only have so much time. The days, after all, are evil (Ephesians 5:16) and short (Psalm 103:15).

We are more obligated to speak to some people (e.g., family members) than others. And I should qualify that, as a pastor, I offer my time to the members of my church regardless of where I perceive them to be on racial matters. But this list still offers a helpful rubric for considering how far to go, even in these conversations.

Fruit 9: Even if we did know what to say at times, we'd be afraid to say it (in other words, we wear the mask!) because . . .

Root 9: We fear receiving or inflicting pain.

It seems more Christians than ever want to get issues of race and racism right. We don't want to make them worse; we don't want to be insensitive. And when we see the weight of these matters (as discussed above) and the harm that can happen if we drop that weight, we tremble. We retreat. Or, if we do talk, we speak mainly with those with whom we feel safe.

The truth is that it's not hard to talk about race *with everyone*. We likely have people we feel safe enough talking about these matters with because we trust them. We feel as if they will be nice to us and give our sincere questions and qualms a fair hearing. But outside of that group, we don't have the same confidence.

Have you ever felt that you'd love to share your honest opinion about a racial matter, but you didn't feel like you could? Maybe you've felt like the race conversation is often just about black and white and we could really benefit from talking about Asian or Native American or Hispanic struggles, but you didn't feel safe to share this thought. Maybe you've tried to share your thoughts before, and the conversation blew up. You were met with defensiveness or disregard. Maybe you were called names, even by your friends. Beloved, ask yourself, who would want to sign up for that again? Who wants to enter a conversation in which there is a lot of criticism and little grace?

What Can We Do? Take It Easy.

We will make the work of entering these conversations easier *if we go easier on each other.* In Titus 3, Paul instructs Titus to remind his people to avoid quarreling and be gentle toward everyone (see also Ephesians 4:1–3). When it comes to these conversations, we have two options—we can outlaw them, or we can lower the temperature in them.[12] Be cool, and take it easy (Proverbs 17:27).

Fruit 10: We don't think well about race and racism because . . .

Root 10: We haven't been taught well.

One reason that conversations about race are so hard is because too many American evangelicals lack thinking with biblical nuance. Sadly, when it comes to using our God-given brains, evangelicals often have only two speeds. For the evangelical, if something is not essential for salvation, it's often regarded as unimportant. Issues, then, are either of speed 1: ultimate importance, or speed 2: no importance. Os Guinness reflects on the sin and scandal of evangelicals refusing to love the Lord with their *minds*: "American evangelicals therefore characteristically display an impatience with the difficult, an intolerance of complexity, and a poor appreciation of the long-term and disciplined. Correspondingly, we often demonstrate a tendency toward the simplistic, especially in the form of slogans or overly simple either/or solutions."[13]

This either/or mental proclivity is why evangelicals often pit two good things against each other (e.g., evangelism versus justice, the spiritual versus the social, man's responsibility versus God's sovereignty, etc.). It's why we often see those who disagree with us as a part of the faithful *or* as a full-blown heretic—we only have two speeds.

And I think the blame for this kind of thinking is largely to be laid at pastors' feet. Why do our people not think deeply about the sin of racism? Is it because we teach on the need to confess and battle lust and greed, but not partiality? As a pastor, I know how difficult it can be to teach on these matters. To be sure, no pastor should be an armchair sociologist or political pundit—and it is easier to become one of these than one might think. And yet we shouldn't fall into the other side of the ditch either, the side of complete reticence. Pastors, when it comes to justice, the Bible is not silent. When it comes to the image of God, the Bible is not silent. When it comes to love, the Bible is not silent.

No doubt, we can only say so much—for the more specific we get, the more we are binding consciences to something Scripture may not specify. Yet, pastors, we also have to realize that some of us have wrongly divorced matters of race from discipleship, and we've taught our people to do the same. In doing so, could it be that we've unwittingly, though wrongly, taught our people that Christ's lordship doesn't extend to this area of their lives and understanding, when in fact it does? Could it be that we've wrongly refused to model for our people how to have these conversations, and they have floundered for it?

What Can We Do? Get a Ten-Speed Bike.

In some sense, the suggested action items above will help you think better, but a crucial one is this: find a friend who thinks well and who disagrees with you. That kind of friend is like a ten-speed bike your thinking can ride around on and be improved. A white pastor comes to mind who once had very strong thoughts on reparations—that is, until he spent time with a group of black pastors. Diverse friends enrich thinking, and we're simply going to have to have more speeds than "heretic" and "faithful" if we're going to speak with each other. We must recognize that someone disagreeing with our perspective does not necessarily make them a Marxist or a racist. Nor does someone disagreeing with our perspective necessarily mean they are disagreeing with God.

Fruit 11: Not all of us want to have a conversation because . . .

Root 11: We don't want to hear it.

It's tempting to think that there's a perfect way to talk about race, and if we just used the right words, then our problems would be solved and we would all get along. Years of having these conversations have shown me that this ideal is but a fantasy of the uninitiated. To be sure, there are better and worse ways to talk about race (hence, this book!). But sadly, in some cases, it does not matter how biblically faithful one's presentation is, there are some folks who, when it comes to race and racism, simply do not want to hear it. They don't want to hear the truth. Maybe it's because they don't like their narrative of the world being disrupted. Maybe it's because they wrongly assume that unity means we can never disagree. Maybe it's because people's minds are really hard to change. People usually believe what they believe for a reason. The civil-rights leader and theologian C. Hebert Oliver noted, "The ideas that are expressed in institutions are not easily arrived at, and therefore not easily changed. Ideas easily acquired are easily lost. . . . The permanence of these institutions makes them defy change, and they refuse to give ground without a struggle."[14] Whatever the case, if sinful stubbornness is our problem, the action step is simple.

What Can We Do? Repent.

Friend, if we've been hard-hearted about issues of race, we can either dig in our heels or turn our eyes toward Jesus. In him we can find a Savior who forgives our callousness, a keeper who shores up our insecurity, and a friend who welcomes us despite our pushback. There is hope for us yet to repent. The Holy Spirit is not done with us yet. That's another reason why conversations about race among Christians can be so hard—we're still works in progress. We're still being sanctified, and sanctification can be disorienting. We change. Our friends change. We change at different rates and on different topics. That change can happen without our even realizing it. We look up and feel like we're in a room we once knew, yet we no longer know where the walls are. But we are safe. Why? Because, though the walls may be gone, Jesus is not.

Questions for Reflection and Discussion

1. Which of the reasons for why it is so hard to talk about race across color lines resonated with you most? Why?
2. Which reason did you most disagree with, if any? Why?
3. What reasons would you add to this list? Why would you add those reasons?

Why Is It So Hard to Talk about
Race across Color Lines?

Throughout this book, I've listed (some) reasons why it's so hard to talk about race. Here is a condensed version of that list.

IT'S SO HARD TO TALK ABOUT RACE BECAUSE . . .

- Of sin.
- Race and racism are broad topics.
- Race and racism are complex topics.
- Race and racism are painful topics.
- Race and racism aren't painful topics for everyone. (That is, we have different experiences.)
- We legitimately disagree about how to apply Scripture to the challenges of race.
- Our churches are largely segregated.
- We're trying to have in-person conversations online.
- We don't know what to say.
- Even if we do know what to say, we are afraid to say it.
- We don't think well. (At times, we think more with our political base than our Bibles).
- We haven't been taught well.
- Some folks don't want to hear it when it comes to race. Period.
- Satan hates our churches, and stoking racial strife has been one of his greatest victories in marring their witness.
- We're all being sanctified at different rates on different issues.
- Some of us are in the most diverse church we've ever been in, and that's new for us.

- We speak unclearly, and so we speak past one another.
- We don't give our conversation partner a fair shot because we don't think they'll actually listen or change.
- We are too sensitive.
- We hear things people aren't saying, and we say things people aren't hearing.
- We're often tone-deaf.
- We speak as if no racial progress has been made or we speak as if there is not still work left to do.
- We speak as if someone must agree with us on everything to be a faithful Christian.
- Sometimes, we care more about the things that divide us instead of the Savior that unites us.

This seems like an overwhelming list, but praise God, there is still hope for us in Christ.

CHAPTER 9

HOW SHOULD WE TALK ABOUT RACE ACROSS COLOR LINES?

"These are the things that you shall do: Speak the truth to one another; render in your gates judgments that are true and make for peace; do not devise evil in your hearts against one another, and love no false oath, for all these things I hate, declares the LORD.*"*

—ZECHARIAH 8:16–17

The darkness is ripe for the church to be a beacon.

—KEITH PLUMMER[1]

'll never forget that truck. I was driving on the highway and happened to pull up behind it. Pinned to the back of it was a weathered, neon orange sign that warned: "CONSTRUCTION VEHICLE: NOT RESPONSIBLE FOR DAMAGE IF FOLLOWED." And I thought to myself, "How is that fair!? He gets to drive without worrying about what comes in his wake!" Then, as I was sitting self-righteously behind my steering wheel, I realized something: that truck is a pretty good picture of my mouth. I wonder if you'd say the same.

I fear sometimes in our conversations about race, we're like this construction truck. We mean to be building something and doing good work. But we're plowing through conversations as if we're not responsible for any damage that follows.

In the last chapter, I gave some practical tips to help us speak more helpfully about race. If chapter 8 was about practical help, this one is more about which posture would be helpful to embrace in our conversations. How should we steer our conversations about race?

As with chapters 7 and 8, we could answer our question simply. *How should Christians talk about race across color lines? Like Christians.* But, as with those previous two chapters, I won't leave you with just the simple answer. Let's go deeper. Here are twelve answers for how Christians should talk about race across color lines.

1. Biblically (2 Timothy 3:16–17)

Scripture, not our political party and the latest *New York Times* bestseller, is our first and final authority on matters of race. One reason talking about race is so difficult is because the issue is often a political football, and sometimes we side with our base rather than relying on our Bibles. This ought not be. We should, above all, speak biblically about race across color lines.

This point has three implications. First, it reminds us that we're not just out to have conversations, but conversations according to God's Word. It's tempting to think that unity is the goal, but we want unity in the truth. J. I. Packer wrote, "We are not entitled to infer from the fact that a group of people are drawing nearer to each other that any of them is drawing nearer to the truth."[2]

Second, because the Bible doesn't speak exhaustively on every issue, there isn't a straight line from Scripture to each of our conclusions about race and racism. This means we must be charitable with other believers who see complex issues differently than we do.

Third, if evangelicals give greater weight to the Bible in our conversations about race, we will use more biblical language in our conversations. As much as we can, let's use and define that language. This won't resolve every problem, but it will provide more common ground.

2. Humbly (Philippians 2:1–11)

You may not have it all figured out when it comes to talking about race, but there is one thing you can have. It will change how you speak, listen, and love. What is it?

Humility.

Christians should speak humbly about racial matters. Give me the humble cat over the racial know-it-all any day! Philippians 2 offers great instruction on how to be humble—counting others more significant than yourself and not looking only to your own interests but also to the interests of others. That means when we come to this conversation, we can't just say, "This is hard for me, so I'm out." Humility will often require us to be uncomfortable.

And we need boldness to do this. Humility requires boldness because it exposes us to risk as we lower ourselves and put others' needs before our own. Being humble in these conversations means we admit that we may be wrong or that we may have messed up. It means we stop showing up to the table as if we have everything to say and nothing to learn.

3. Locally (Acts 20:28; 1 Peter 5:2)

Some of us need to realize that we argue more with the caricature in our mind than the person in our presence. In other words, we project a national conversation onto one person and speak to them as if they hold every belief we find objectionable. But we shouldn't do this, nor do we need to. We may not be able to influence our entire denomination or nation, but we can influence the people at our dinner tables, on our school boards, and in our churches. Let us talk with real people where God has placed us. Beloved, don't take things that are happening nationally and necessarily assume they're happening in your church or home. Address the problems that are happening locally. Have conversations with your community without projecting everyone else's problems onto it.

4. Kindly (Colossians 4:6; Ephesians 4:32)

"Let your speech always be gracious" (Colossians 4:6). No one's sin toward us can ever justify our sin toward them. What's more, these days, when everyone is outraged about everything, kindness is radical. How did Joseph speak to his brothers, who sold him into slavery? "'Do not fear; I will provide for you and your little ones.' Thus he comforted them and spoke *kindly* to them" (Genesis 50:21).

5. Prayerfully (Ephesians 6:18)

Is there not something in matters of race that should lead us to confession, petition, thanksgiving, or lament? Is there not something that causes us to see the poverty of our own resources and the abundance of God's? Maybe talking to someone else about these matters would be easier if we talked to God more—that is, perhaps we have so much trouble in our conversations because we pray so little about them. The Bible commands prayer. Church history commends prayer. Pastors know about prayer. And Christians agree on prayer. That is, we may disagree on a host of issues regarding race, but all Christians agree we should rely on God in prayer.

Given that I'm the founder of United? We Pray, I'm naturally going to wax on the point of prayer for a minute. So many people get themselves tied up in knots about how their church can better address racial issues. Here is a simple way: pray about them. Get on your face about them. Have a prayer meeting about them. Pray about them on Sundays publicly. Together. Grab the throne and don't let go until God blesses you. I like what Pastor John Onwuchekwa said:

> The prayer list—not the Sunday service elements, not the preaching style, not even the ethnic makeup of the leadership of the church—is often where the battle for diversity is won or lost. What makes the prayer list is often a reflection of who's praying and whose problems are seen as real, relevant, and important. A friend of mine was a part of a church that refused to pray for anything related to Mike Brown, Trayvon Martin, Eric Gardner . . . or any other African American who was killed at the hands of law enforcement, because those issues were "too politicized" and would cause division in their church. This frustrated her. She didn't want her church to march on Washington or hang a Black Lives Matter flag from the steeple. She simply wanted them to pray corporately on these matters because she knew they were deeply significant to many of the minorities in the church. That church failed to realize something that was apparent to the early church: fostering unity and diversity involves more than including cultural elements in a Sunday service; it involves showing solidarity with minorities in the struggles they face. . . . The battle for diversity is still won or lost here today. Diversity is more about priorities than programs. And a church prays for what it prioritizes. [Pastors,] your prayer lists essentially serve as price tags on current events and church concerns—assigning value or diminishing it. Therefore, don't populate the prayer list in isolation. Populate the list with the concerns of all the flock.[3]

And given his influence on my life, I must quote Francis Grimké at length. His sermon "God and Prayer as Factors in the Struggle," has changed my life. I stumbled across it after some racial tragedy (I can't remember which one). I had been tired of pontificating on social media, and I was also tired of reading everyone else's pontifications.

So I put down my phone and did a radical thing—I read a book. Specifically, I read the collection of Grimké's sermons that I recommend in the resources section in chapter 11. Here is one quote on Christian slaves and their commitment to pray that has never left me:

> When they were hoeing in the cotton field, when the crack of the overseer's whip was sounding in their ears, when their backs were smarting under the lash of the hard taskmaster, when they stood upon the auction block, when families were broken up— the father going in one direction, the mother in another, and the children in still another—there went up from their bleeding hearts the cry to heaven, "How long, O Lord, how long?" Every day, every night, almost every hour in every day, the cry of their bleeding hearts was poured into the ear of Heaven. And I believe, as mighty as were the other influences, there was none more potential than this. Prayer was their only weapon at that time, and how mightily did they wield it.

Grimké goes on to say,

> Lawless ruffians may keep the Negro away from the polls by shotguns; and by unrighteous laws and intimidation may shut him out of first-class cars, but there is no power by which all the combined forces of evil in the South can keep the Negro from approaching the throne of grace.

And so he concluded,

> It is a solemn thing when millions of souls, however poor and humble they may be, carry their appeal from man's injustice to the bar of the Almighty. It is a serious matter for a nation when any body of people, however few, betake themselves not to revolt, but to prayer.[4]

If suffering slaves prayed like this, how much more should we?

6. Justly (Proverbs 3:27; James 4:17)

We should talk about race justly, and the reason I mention this is because it's easy to have a negative goal when it comes to race conversations. Many believers simply do not want to be racist. But we don't just want to negatively avoid what we shouldn't be. Positively, we want to be advocates for those who don't have a voice (Proverbs 31:8). Positively, we want to speak what is right, not just avoid speaking what is wrong. How does the psalmist put it? "The mouth of the righteous utters wisdom, and his tongue speaks justice" (Psalm 37:30). Silence can often be wisdom, yes, but silence can also be sinful (Ecclesiastes 3:7).

7. Patiently (1 Corinthians 13:4)

The first characteristic of love listed in 1 Corinthians 13 is that it is *patient*. So let's not listen to one another only to respond or to correct, but to understand. And understanding usually takes time. If you're struggling to extend that time, keep in mind that there was a time when, on a given topic, you were in the dark and ignorant, and people were patient with you. Remember that. Or get around an older saint in your church and witness their patience—and learn.

8. Carefully (Proverbs 12:18; 14:15; James 1:19)

Given how complicated conversations about race can be, refinement and precision are often needed. Yet most of us blunder in these conversations. What does the wise writer of Proverbs tell us about using our words? "There is one whose rash words are like sword thrusts, but the tongue of the wise brings healing" (Proverbs 12:18). There's a reason why surgeons operate with scalpels and not swords. We need to drop our weaponized, rash language and pick up careful, healing speech. Another aspect of careful speech is clarity. Clear speech is often careful speech. Paul wrote what he hoped people could fully understand (2 Corinthians 1:13). May we do the same when we speak of race.

9. Impartially (James 2:1)

Speaking wisely means that we also must speak consistently. We can't just be concerned with the problems of the "other" side. We have to be willing to admit that "our" side might have some problems too. And we will build trust with the people we disagree with if we point out those problems as well. We should not fear that in admitting "our" side's faults, we are ceding too much ground to the "other" side. The truth is not something we *use* to protect our interests or party. Rather, the truth is something we *tell*, regardless of who needs to hear it. We ought to speak the truth clearly, consistently, impartially.

10. Truthfully (Exodus 20:16; Proverbs 29:5)

"A lying tongue hates its victims, and a flattering mouth works ruin," says Proverbs 26:28. Tell the truth, beloved. Leave the results to God. If people are going to bristle in our conversations about race, let it be because they are convicted by the truth, not frustrated by our deceit.

11. Realistically (Mark 6:31)

Some of us speak as if we expect to change overnight the issues the nation has been wrestling with for centuries. Be sure, as you speak, that you're not trying to sprint a marathon. Take breaks. We are in a battle, and as in any battle, there are times to retreat, recover, or even retire and let other parts of the troop push forward. Put differently, don't be consumed by this conversation. Be consumed by Jesus. Spend time with Jesus. He's coming back again, isn't he?

12. Hopefully (Romans 15:13)

Being a realist doesn't mean being a pessimist. Beloved, let's speak with hope. There is a lot of talk these days about being prophetic in our conversations about race. I'm all for that, but I fear that people have reduced the prophetic task merely to confrontation. But the prophets didn't just condemn; they also comforted. They comforted God's people specifically by giving hope—the hope of restoration and redemption. Ezra 5:2 says the prophets were with the people of God, *supporting them* in their work. And as much as we can, we should support one another. Brothers and sisters, Jesus is alive, and that means that one day racism will be dead. Let's speak as if that's true—that is, let's speak hopefully.

That's it. There's no secret sauce here. All we've tried to do in this book is think with our Bibles about how we can speak Christianly on these matters. May God give us grace to do so.

I have hope that he will.

And it's because of this hope that we have one more scene in our story.

We began our story with Hunter and Darius. You'll remember that the year prior to Malachi Brewers's case, Hunter had tried to reach out to Darius to talk about another killing, JaVari Dupree's. When they met, Hunter and Darius didn't have a great conversation. Hunter was a bit naive and tone-deaf in his questions, and Darius was a bit rude. The good news is that the Holy Spirit is more than a bit alive. And so we return back to our story.

We left off with Brother Mack's demeaning conversation with Darius in the LRBC parking lot. Hunter had overheard the whole exchange. What will happen next? Will Hunter and Darius attempt to have another conversation, as Hunter's wife suggested? Will Pastor Bruce hear of Brother Mack's words and step in? Will Anna Beth somehow confront her dad? Let's see.

CHAPTER 10

CLOSING THE SCENE

Forgiveness

> Put on then, as God's chosen ones, holy and
> beloved, compassionate hearts, kindness, humility,
> meekness, and patience, bearing with one another and,
> if one has a complaint against another, forgiving each
> other; as the Lord has forgiven you, so you also must
> forgive. And above all these put on love, which binds
> everything together in perfect harmony.

—COLOSSIANS 3:12–14

> Crises are political only until they become
> personal.

—ELAINA PLOTT[1]

Hunter sat through the prayer meeting, his mind racing. He
could hardly focus on anything during it; he was too shocked.
Or disturbed. Or disgusted. He didn't know the word, but he knew
what he had seen and heard in the parking lot, and he couldn't shake
it. He wouldn't shake it. *How could Brother Mack say that to Darius?*
he kept wondering to himself. *How could I not speak up for Darius?*

Darius—Hunter's friend, brother, and fellow deacon—somehow, by God's grace, got up in front of the church and gave his word of hope anyway.

"He crushed it," Hunter's wife leaned over and whispered to him as Darius left the stage. "Darius absolutely crushed it."

The service ended, and Hunter hardly remembered the drive home, the lunch afterward, or the fact that Darius hadn't answered his text about meeting this week. Hunter knew he had to say something to Darius, but he wasn't sure what, how, or when—especially given the week Darius had had. Nonetheless, he got out his phone.

He had a message from Darius.

"Shoot," Hunter said under his breath. "I missed this."

Darius's text said,

Hey, bro, let me circle back with you about getting together. I did just shoot you a quick email though. Would be good for you to read before we meet up.

Hunter opened his email so fast his wife thought something was wrong. She asked him what was up, but he couldn't hear her. He just read.

Darius Lowry <d.lowry@mail.com>
To: Hunter Caulkins <hunterc@mail.com>
Subject: Apology
Date: October 4, 2020

Hey bro,

Before we meet up, I wanted to say I'm sorry. And I'm sorry for something I should've apologized for a long time ago but didn't, and that's how I spoke to you last year when we tried to have a similar conversation to the one I imagine you're hoping to have soon. I called you and the other deacons white supremacists. I spoke harshly. I shut you down. And you were trying to help. Bruce's sermon today convicted me, and I need to ask for your forgiveness, brother. I don't want to have a conversation like that again. Not with you. Not with anyone. And after what Mack said to me in the parking lot, I'm convinced—this has just got to stop. We have to be better about how we speak to one another on these things—and that includes myself. Will you please forgive me, Hunter?

Imma add one more thing, not as a defense but as an explanation of how minorities can speak out of their pain sometimes. Maybe this will help our next conversation, if and when it happens. (I say if and when b/c at the present moment, I'm just not sure I have the strength for it. I trust you get that. I hope you do.)

Anyway, man, I want you to know that I cried. When I got off the stage, after I gave my lil spiel, I went downstairs in an empty office and straight-up cried. I really cannot believe what Brother Mack said to me.

Hunter, I wish I could describe how it feels to be on the receiving end of that kind of speech. I wish I could describe how it feels when a minority speaks up about race and members of the majority greet you with criticism, not compassion; with hostility, not humility; with a warning, not a welcome. These responses are disturbing, divisive, and destructive—but sadly, unsurprising. Yet they still hurt. And it's a double dose of pain when these greetings come from folks who profess Christ! Hunter, hear me: I'm not saying there's no place for criticism. This isn't emotional blackmail.

Rather, this is living in light of history. This is having sympathy, compassion, a tender heart, a humble mind (1 Peter 3:8). This is Loving Your Neighbor 101.

Of course, there's a place for criticism. But, Hunter, there is a BIGGER place for listening. Lamenting. Trusting, not threatening. Which one will you live in—the bigger or the smaller place? As you've now seen and heard, the latter is where some loud members of the majority live—with a cold, callous, critical spirit.

But I want to live in the bigger place, bro. I'm thankful for our white brothers and sisters who live there too. In that place there is love, mercy, and grace. And guess what? There is still room in the inn.

And even if those who are mean and loud and oddly defensive don't come in, we who live in the bigger place will keep extending love, mercy, and grace. We will love our enemies, win them in the process, and ours will be a double victory. And as we go about that work, we will pray folks see the damage their words and actions inflict. And we'll pray to the One who judges justly; the One who is not slow as some count slowness; the One who will bring every careless word into the light.

Bro, this email is getting long, so let me wrap up with one last thing, and only because you've asked how you can be learning about these matters. Hunter, I love running with you. Really, I do. The reason I insist on us running together, though, is not because I'm a health nut or enjoy our fellowship (though that's true). It's because I'm scared. I'm scared to run in our neighborhood by myself. I'm not trying to scare anyone else and wind up dead and have Jackson's dad be another horrifying story on the news. I don't want to think a second more about it. So let me end this note here. I pray it's helpful, and again, please forgive me.

All love to you and your beautiful family,
—D

Hunter's wife was really concerned now because tears were streaming down Hunter's face.

"Hun-ter. Tell. Me. What's. Wrong!" she shouted. She was sure he had lost his job, or one of his parents had died and he was hearing about it in some weird way, or something like that. Hunter simply looked up from his phone at her.

"I've got to go talk to him," he said, as he stood up and made his way to the door. "I've got to talk to him now."

"Who?!" Hunter's wife asked. "Who are you going to talk to?" But her words were too slow for a man running to repair. Hunter had already left the room. He got in his car and drove faster than he had driven to church that morning. All the while, he only had one question he kept asking himself in disbelief: "Why on earth is Darius apologizing to *me*?"

Hunter arrived at his destination and screeched his car to a stop. He got out of the car, walked right up to the door, and knocked. The door opened.

"Hey, Hunter!" Brother Mack said. "I'm surprised to see you, buddy, paying me a visit on the Lord's Day. What's up?"

Hunter had no smile on his face. He stood there with restraint and began speaking. "I need to talk to you about how you spoke to Darius in the parking lot today, brother, and I need to talk to you now."

—The End—

Questions for Reflection and Discussion

1. What do you think Hunter said to Brother Mack? How do you think Brother Mack responded?
2. You'll remember Jackson and Clay from the opening scene. As regards race, what kind of world do you think they'll grow up in? What kind of world would you like them to grow up in? How can you, by God's grace, be a part of making that kind of world?

CHAPTER 11

WHEN THE NEXT RACIAL TRAGEDY HAPPENS, WHAT CAN YOU DO?

I f you wanted a resolution to every one of our friends' stories, I'm
sorry to disappoint. The truth is, though, in this fallen world, not
all stories have a happy ending. We can hope for the best, and I'll
leave you to imagine what happens with Samantha Lee and Anna
Beth, whether Jane sticks with her job and LRBC—and of course,
what happens with Darius. Does he stay at LRBC? Does he follow
José Luis to his new church? Who knows?

The time has come to finish our work here. We've gotten in
our truck and thought about how we can more responsibly drive
on the road of racial conversations. Now it's time to actually go
somewhere. We are, Lord willing, better equipped to *do something*,
and sadly, I'm confident we'll have plenty of opportunity to do so,
because racial tragedies aren't going away. The next viral video of a
racial tragedy won't be the first of its kind, and unfortunately, until
the Lord returns, I fear it won't be the last. As Christians, we know
something is wrong in this fallen order. As Christians, we know
racial strife has an expiration date. Until then, *what can you do?*

It's a good question. Dear brothers and sisters who want to
love their neighbors are asking it. That word *can* in the question is

crucial. We're not saying, "thou *must* do such and such." Yet while folks appreciate their conscience not being wrongly bound, they are often wondering what, positively, they *can* do. *"What can I do, especially when racial tragedy strikes?"* Here are twenty-six suggestions.

1. **Pray.** By yourself. With other saints. Pray for structural change. Pray for individual change. Pray to have the same moral clarity today that you have on past evils like slavery. Pray for the oppressed. Pray for the oppressor. Pray for your enemies, whomever you perceive them to be. However you pray, whatever you pray, just pray. Weep. Lament. Be angry and do not sin. Put Jehoshaphat's prayer on your lips: "We do not know what to do, but our eyes are on you" (2 Chronicles 20:12).

2. **Discern whether it's wise for you to watch the tragedy.** I make this point mostly with minorities in mind. My guess is that if you're reading this, especially in the wake of a racial tragedy, you've already seen a viral video (or whatever its equivalent would be). But consider if watching future videos of tragedies is wise for you. You may feel like you need to watch or re-watch a video, but that's not necessarily true. Doing so may cause you unnecessary depression. Exercise your freedom in Christ. You may be emotionally or spiritually tapped. Not everyone is equally equipped to dive into each tragedy. Pray for wisdom and ask for counsel as to whether watching would be good for you. We don't want to ignore suffering, but neither do we want to immerse our hearts in it (Proverbs 4:23). Then . . .

3. **Pray some more.**

4. **Study what happened.** If you do decide to look further into a tragedy, read the most credible sources you can on the matter. Don't tweet before you seek information. Take your time in doing this. There's no rush.

5. **Pray some more.**

6. **Examine yourself, and repent if necessary.** One kind of prayer is especially helpful—confession. See if there is any false way, any hatred, any prejudice within you. Confess it to the Lord. Ask the Lord to forgive your hidden faults and your secret sins (Psalm 19:12; 90:8).

7. **Pray some more.**

8. **Educate yourself on the topic of race.** Before seeking what you can do, study what has been done. That is, do some homework on how we got to this present racial moment. People often ask me what books they can be reading about race. Please see the chart at the end of the chapter for my suggestions.

9. **Pray some more.**

10. **Be okay with not being able to fix everything.** Too often when we ask, "What can I do?" we're essentially asking, "How can I fix it?" Sometimes, however, the point isn't to fix something, but to faithfully endure it as we groan along with the rest of creation, for groaning is inescapable until glory. One ugly fact of a fallen world is this: not everything can be fixed. Nevertheless, we can rest in this truth: our job is not to completely eradicate the world of racism; it is to faithfully follow the One who will. And vengeance and perfect justice belong to him. He will judge, fully and finally, and there will be no miscarriage of justice with his gavel. You either do agree with me about this or you will. Of course, I'm not saying that we shouldn't seek temporal justice now, however imperfect, but we can rest, knowing that perfect justice will—not *can* or *may*, but *will* come.

11. **Pray some more.**

12. **Think about what you can do in your specific calling in life.** Are you a pastor? What might this mean for how you speak to your church? Are you a homemaker? How might you teach your kids? (The afterword may be of help to you parents.) All of us have different roles and networks. We'll

have to *think* about how to use them. Racism is a monster with many heads, and there are many faithful ways to go after it. Not all of us have the same role, and that's okay.

13. **Pray some more.**

14. **Regardless of how you feel about a tragedy, reach out to a brother or sister who may be grieving.** This step could get messy, and why wouldn't it? After all, love is messy. That said, I think this step is important. Before we elaborate on it, I want to clarify the larger point behind this step. The point isn't to contact someone for the sake of contacting them. I say this especially for white brothers and sisters who may be wondering, "When a racial tragedy strikes, should I contact that one, random friend I haven't spoken to in years?" Maybe, but probably not. The point isn't to check a box, then move on in life. Rather, the point is to help foster an environment (especially in our churches) where tenderness and sympathy on racial matters is normalized, expected, and valued. Checking in with folks you know and love is a wonderful way to build up that environment, for when one part of the body suffers, all suffer (1 Corinthians 12:26).

When you reach out to folks, recognize that not everyone will want to be contacted or will have the same opinion (though some will). When you reach out, don't demand a response. When you reach out, don't ask the person what you can do or ask them to explain all of what's going on to you. That means not leading with a general question like, "Hey, how are you doing with this?" Such a question may put pressure on the person to describe the indescribable.

When six Asian women were shot in Atlanta in March 2021, I checked in with some Asian brothers and sisters I know saying, "I don't know how these shootings hit you, and you don't have to tell me or even respond. But I love you, I'm praying, and I'm here if you want to talk. No pressure."

I share this not to boast but to provide an example. And you know what? My Asian brothers and sisters blessed me with powerful conversations.

You'll notice that this point about reaching out to folks isn't the first action step on this list. That's intentional. It's not because I'm trying to add another rule to a conversation that has so much law and so little grace. It's not because I expect imperfect people to speak perfectly. It's because taking some of the above actions before you ask your question will help you ask in a more informed, loving way.

15. **Pray some more.**

16. **Believe.** When a minority tells you about their experience, believe them. That is, give them the benefit of the doubt. Don't put them on trial and make them justify their pain, which does nothing but double it. Believe them.

17. **Pray some more.**

18. **Keep listening.** It's easy to be like Job's friends during tragedies. One way to keep from being like them is to close your mouth. You want to sin less? Speak less, and simply listen to that person speaking to you (Proverbs 10:19). The pressure will be on you to say something. Don't give in. Just because you tweet something doesn't mean you care; just because you don't tweet something doesn't mean you don't. Live before God as your audience, no one else.

19. **Pray some more.**

20. **Support those already doing something.** Instead of reinventing the wheel, as we're prone to do when asking, "What can I do?" see who is already doing something.[1] How can you get behind their efforts? Can you support them financially? Can you support them in prayer? This point helps us to see that we're not in this battle against racism alone. We need not only ask, "What can *I* do?" but also "What can *we* do?"

21. **Pray some more.**

22. **Get involved locally.** One effect of social media is that it makes us want to be omni-present, but are there flesh-and-blood people suffering around you whom you can get to know? Whom you can serve regularly? Is there a neighborhood you're tempted to walk or drive by that you could somehow love? Is there a church in that neighborhood you can encourage or support? Is there a local high school or crisis pregnancy center you can help? Let us not be those who are known digitally but not locally.

23. **Pray some more.**

24. **Remember, rest in, and keep sharing the gospel.** Christian, you have something so many people don't—hope in Christ. We want this world to be as good as it can be, but we know that even if it was, there is still a better world coming—one that lasts forever, one ruled by a King who died to save his people. Share that hope.

25. **Pray some more.**

26. **Commit** to repeating some combination of the steps listed above when there's not a high-profile racial tragedy in the news. We don't want to be merely reactive to problems, but to proactively cut them off.

Brothers and sisters, the next racial tragedy need not catch you flat-footed. I pray this list of ways you can begin responding is helpful for you and your family. And it's families I want to talk about as we close this book. Remember Clay Caulkins and Jackson Lowry from the beginning of our story? Friends who read this book in manuscript form said I must circle back to them. My friends were right.

While not everyone reading this book is going to be a parent, all of us will have an opportunity to speak to the next generation. If you're looking for guidance on how to do that when it comes to race, I have some wise friends whom I would like you to meet and hear from in the afterword.

Ten Books on Race to Begin With (and Some Other Resources Too)

RESOURCE	LENGTH/GENRE
The Bible!	There's no better book. Passages to consider and questions you could ask in a small group: • Genesis 1:26–28 and Acts 17:26 • What implications does being made in God's image have for conversations about race? How many races are there? • Acts 6:1–7; 7:19 and Matthew 28:19 • What do we see about how ethnicities can be and should be treated in these passages? • Genesis 3:15; Ephesians 2:14–15; 1 Peter 2:9–10 • How might the truth of a "chosen race" factor into our racial discussions? How should we talk about this truth?
How to Think: A Survival Guide for a World at Odds by Alan Jacobs	A short book, and while not explicitly about race, it will help prepare you to think about racial issues.
Racism and World Evangelism by Tom Skinner	An hour-long address, given at Urbana in 1970, that can be used by a small group to listen to and discuss.
Narrative of the Life of Frederick Douglass: an American Slave by Frederick Douglass	A short autobiography by one of the most remarkable humans to ever live. Douglass's firsthand account of slavery and his condemnation of false, American Christianity is gripping.
The Negro, His Rights and Wrongs, the Forces for Him and against Him by Francis Grimké	A small collection of sermons preached in 1898 by an African American pastor in Washington, DC.
The Warmth of Other Suns: The Epic Story of America's Great Migration by Isabel Wilkerson	A book as good as it is long. While not explicitly Christian, the book is masterful in its education about an era of history many Americans have not considered—the Great Migration. If you're looking to understand the racial landscape of our country, start with this moving history on early twentieth-century America.

American Apartheid: Segregation and the Making of the Underclass by Douglas S. Massey and Nancy A. Denton	This is the densest read on this list, but it's worth the work. It's not a Christian book, but the data and history it details is harrowing. It would be good to read after *The Warmth of Other Suns*, as it focuses on late twentieth-century America.
Race and Place: How Urban Geography Shapes the Journey to Reconciliation by David Leong	This is a good read for those trying to wrap their minds around structural racism. This book emphasizes the role of the local church as part of the solution. It focuses on the racial layout of present-day America.
Beyond Racial Gridlock: Embracing Mutual Responsibility by George Yancey	The best book I know of on all of us embracing our responsibility in the race conversation. This work is deeply Christian.
Consumed by Hate, Redeemed by Love: How a Violent Klansman Became a Champion of Racial Reconciliation by Thomas A. Tarrants	How does someone become radicalized when it comes to race? Come hear firsthand from a former Ku Klux Klansman whom the Lord radically saved.
Divided by Faith: Evangelical Religion and the Problem of Race in America by Michael O. Emerson and Christian Smith	While it does not major on solutions, this seminal book offers a piercing diagnosis of the evangelical racial landscape in America. You can see the sequel, *United by Faith*, for more of Emerson's thoughts on solutions.
Meals from Mars: A Parable of Prejudice and Providence by Ben Sciacca	A short, easy-to-read novel that's a good introduction for teenagers thinking about race.

AFTERWORD

LITTLE MASKS— TALKING ABOUT RACE WITH YOUR KIDS

"Let the little children come to me."

—MATTHEW 19:14

I have a dream that my four little children will one day live in a nation where they will not be judged by the color of their skin but by the content of their character.

—MARTIN LUTHER KING JR.[1]

"You are beautiful." These are three words I try to say every day to my baby girl. I hold her puffy, precious cheeks. I look her in those big brown eyes. And I remind her that *she is beautiful.*

This is a message black parents have felt compelled to say to their boys and girls in a world that tells them they're ugly. I remember a black pastor in a predominantly white church talking about why he had to leave for another church. His little black girl was being made fun of by her friends, who were white, because her nose was "too

171

wide." It killed my friend that his little girl didn't have any friends to play with who looked like her. I could relate. I recall my daughter receiving a plush chair covered in Disney princesses who were all white. I didn't want her to internalize the message that to be a princess, she had to be white, or that her hair had to look a certain way!

And so I began regularly preaching my three-word sermon: "You are beautiful." I began a short catechism with my daughter, just as my mother had used to indoctrinate my sisters. "Whose image are you made in?" Mom would ask. And now my three-year-old girl answers the same question. "God" she says, often in a rote way. But hey, I'm just trying to pack the truth in now and let the Holy Spirit unpack it later.

Why am I going on about children? Because our story began with them. As I wrote about Jackson Lowry and Clay Caulkins, I had several questions. What would overhearing the television news or their parents' conversations do to these tender hearts? What kind of world do we want them to grow up in? How can we dream for our kids and instruct them regarding race in a biblically faithful and hopeful way?

These are questions on many parents' minds. We want to talk with our kids, but some of us are unsure of what to say and how to speak. And you know what? So am I. My children are still little, so I've asked some older, wiser, and godlier friends if they would share their wisdom on how to speak with kids about race. After my friends address us, I'll conclude with a prayer for the next generation.

Counsel from Karen Ellis, Courtney Reissig, Bobby Scott, and Ray Ortlund

Karen Ellis: Teaching the Diversity of the Promise

Karen Ellis serves as director for the Center for the Study of the Bible and Ethnicity at Reformed Theological Seminary, Atlanta. She and her husband Carl have two adult children and one granddaughter.

God has promised to make and keep a people for himself from every tongue, tribe, and nation. This means that every people group in God's world carries intentional, redemptive purpose: to display God's glory to a fallen world, to gather his people from every nation, tongue, and tribe, and to proclaim the redemptive work of Jesus Christ.

In other words, the biblical genealogies and narratives of God's people aren't just there to give us melodic or meaningful baby names. Those names, and even their locations and the people who inhabited them, point us to the grand story of God's promise and the faithful and unfaithful through whom the story is playing out in history.

At times Scripture arranges our real-life spiritual ancestors in chronological genealogies, and at other times we see lives grafted into the story by their faithful allegiance to the God of Abraham, Isaac, and Jacob through faith in Christ. But all are connected by invisible, infinite, zig-zagging connections that carry history, identity, truth, and meaning for us who have now received the kingdom ball to pass to the next generation. The idea almost foreshadows the Lamb's book of life—perhaps not so much a list of names, but a collection of lives lived in faithful allegiance to the King of kings for the sake of the ingathering of the nations.

One of the most affirming gifts we can give to the generations to come is teaching the worth of each name and tribe that has brought us thus far. When we teach of the promise given to Abraham to birth a people God would bless in order that they might be a blessing to the nations, we can then point young ones to the ultimate fulfillment of the promise commanded from the Savior's resurrected lips:

> Go therefore and make disciples of all nations, baptizing them in the name of the Father and of the Son and of the Holy Spirit, teaching them to observe all that I have commanded you. And behold, I am with you always, to the end of the age. (Matthew 28:19–20)

Suddenly, man-made categories like race, ethnicity, language, and tribe have redemptive value, meaning, and purpose. Parenting and discipling our children and spiritual children affirm God's sovereignty, which proclaims that each of us is intentionally formed and is part of a promise. Our historical placement in time, our culture, our physical appearance, our particular gender, injustices done by and against us, our wounds, and our failures—all of these can be redeemed for Christ's glory and fame.

By recognizing who we are as the people of God—an ingathering of all peoples, each with diverse stories and something to contribute—we tell the watching world that God is doing what he has promised to do. We counter man's perversions and abuses of separating people by category and see God bring transcendent life and meaning to them.

And he promises that he is present with us as we proclaim his truth, to the very end of the age.

Now *that* is good news!

Courtney Reissig: Talking to Your Kids about Race

Courtney Reissig is an author and speaker based in Little Rock, Arkansas. She and her husband Daniel have four children.

My kids still say things that shock me. I suppose that's par for the course. I have four children between the ages of three and eight. They have lots of thoughts and very little filter. Their brains are constantly going, taking in the world around them, making observations, and then spewing those thoughts out to all who will listen.

As a result they often make observations that sound inappropriate. At their ages, they aren't being malicious when they make these statements. They're simply stating facts. They see a child in a wheelchair and they loudly ask why she is in a wheelchair. They try to describe a new friend from school to me and they bluntly mention the color of his skin.

Often when our kids make these quick observations we cringe. We imagine an adult speaking with such candor and project offense or embarrassment onto our children. For white parents of white children (like myself), we are tempted to silence our children, change the subject, or pretend like they are not speaking at that moment. Maybe if we ignore them, no one will notice that they just loudly observed the color of someone else's skin. But I'm starting to think that maybe their observations are actually a sign of health. Instead of seeing these moments of honesty as a time to retreat, I've started taking them as a time to train.

It is important for Christian parents to talk to our children about race, especially when they bring it up. If we don't, they will learn about race by our silence. If we ignore their observations, they will come to think that the differences don't matter. If we silence or shush them, they will infer that talking about race is shameful. We want to raise a generation of children who are not afraid to confront the struggles of racism in our country head-on. And they will only learn to do this if we equip them for the task ahead. They will only learn to do this if we aren't afraid to talk to them about their observations, even when they make us uncomfortable.

When our children ask questions about a person's skin color or make statements about someone who is different from them, we take this as an opportunity to teach them about God's plan for all of creation. When God created Adam and Eve, he says that he created them in his image (Genesis 1:27). This is the foundational truth for why and how we talk to our kids about race. God created every single person in his image. This means that every human being tells the world something of what God is like. Regardless of skin color, developmental ability, or where they are from—people are created in the image of God. At a very young age, children can grasp simple truths like "God made me" and "God made everything." They might not know it in their hearts, but their brains are storing all that information, and Lord willing it will bear fruit in their lives over their lifetime (Psalm 1).

Here's how a conversation might happen in our home.

Son: "Mommy, why is her skin darker than mine?"

Me: "Because God made her that way."

Son: "Why did God make her that way?"

Me: "Because he made every color, and he made every person to tell us what he is like."

Sometimes those questions come at the dinner table, and sometimes they come in the checkout line at the store. No matter when they come, for parents the biggest hurdle is to resist the urge to retreat when our kids make statements that are jarring or seem to be coming out of nowhere. Instead of retreating, we can train. We can teach simple truths about God and what he is like. And we can always pray that God will take our feeble efforts to raise a generation of kids who see the world he has made as a beautiful reflection of his glory.

Bobby Scott: Cross-Cultural and Biblical Teaching

Bobby Scott is pastor of discipleship for Community of Faith Bible Church in South Gate, California. He and his wife Naomi have six children.

I am black, and my wife is Blasian; her father was black, and her mother was Asian. They met while her father was in the Army, stationed in Japan. They fell in love and got married, but that proved to be a problem. Her mother's family disowned her because she married a black man. He died when my wife was young, so she was raised by her ethnically and culturally Japanese mother in a predominantly black neighborhood in Los Angeles and close to her father's black family. My wife and I met in Los Angeles. Later my parents left Los Angeles and moved to Virginia when our six kids were still quite young. So our children grew up spending a lot of time with my wife's mother and experiencing a ton of Japanese culture.

All of my kids look black, and most people assume that my wife is Hispanic. Because of her appearance and the abundance of kids we have, people would ask my wife, "Oh, are you a social worker? Teacher? Nanny?" When they would see my kids with an elderly little Japanese woman, they would assume she ran a day care. But my kids never assumed that families had to be connected by a common phenotype, ethnicity, or culture. They learned that we are all humans (Genesis 1:26–28; Acts 17:26), and this common humanity enables us to build friendships and relationships with people who look like us as well as with those who don't.

We also taught them that sin separates us from God and each other, it separates groups into warring tribes, and it often leads to oppression and racism (Exodus 1:8–16). Genesis 11 explains how humanity collectively rebelled against God to make a name for itself rather than for God. Genesis 10 assumes that we all brought that innate, self-centered, sinful orientation into our tribes (vv. 5, 20, 31), resulting in incurable tribalism. Consciously and subconsciously, our tribal affiliations wield a large influence over us that conforms us to the restraints of groupthink. So we all need a biblically informed worldview regarding race.

Practically, here are two things I advise parents to do. One, read your children the stories of people from different tribes to enable them to vicariously experience life through the eyes of others. This enables them to transcend barriers that leave them ignorant of and indifferent to the struggles of neighbors who are outside their tribe. Second, teach your children the Bible. It tells them their real story and everyone's story. It tells them who they are and why they are. It tells them what is wrong with them and how Christ alone is their solution. It tells them that Jesus died for their sins and rose from the dead to offer them new life. It commands them to turn from their sin to trust in him so they can be born again—born into a new family—a family not defined by ethnicity or culture (1 Peter 2:9) but by God's Spirit and love. Teach them that *the gospel* is primary and that all who are blessed by it must share the message and the love that comes from it with all their neighbors—those who are like them and those who are not.

My wife and I are grateful for our critical role as a means of God's common grace in our children's lives, and we humbly recognize that our children will be who they will be in response to God's sovereign grace. Our youngest is now fifteen and is active in Christian struggles for racial justice. Our oldest is twenty-five, "a-racial," and is marrying her white Christian homeschooled sweetheart. My nineteen-year-old daughter was involved in both her high school's Japanese and Black culture clubs. She now runs track at a conservative, predominantly white Christian university and is an active member of a predominantly Asian church. My twenty-year-old loves all genres of black music and is in the Marine Officer Candidate Training Program in hopes of flying fighter jets. My eighteen-year-old, who is not a believer, chose a Christian college to attend in the fall to study criminal justice to become a police officer (which, due to our present cultural climate, is not a highly sought-after vocation in the black community). My twenty-three-year-old son, also not a believer, attends our predominantly Black church every Sunday. He freely code switches to standard English when he needs to and to African American vernacular around his mainly Black friends. Influenced or shaped by a biblical worldview, my multicultural kids empathize with and relate well to people from all kinds of backgrounds. By God's grace, my kids who are Christians feel free to be the fearfully and wonderfully made and unique image-bearers that God made them to be, and they serve Christ in a range of cultural contexts that reach all of our neighbors.

Ray Ortlund: A Family's Legacy of Waging War against Racism

Ray Ortlund serves as pastor to pastors at Immanuel Church in Nashville, Tennessee, as president of Renewal Ministries, and as a council member for The Gospel Coalition. He and his wife Jani have four adult children and fourteen grandchildren.

My wife Jani and I have been married for fifty years. We have four adult children, all married, and now fourteen grandchildren. It has been a great journey, for which we thank the Lord. But in a way, we wish we could go back and try again. We wish we had been better, wiser, nobler.

You can do better than we have. Your generation is rising up for the glory of Jesus with a fresh, historic opportunity. So, let's think about what any Christian family today, within its range of influence, can do toward replacing the racism of the past with the "one new man" that Jesus is creating (Ephesians 2:15).

1. EXAMPLE

Children learn a lot from watching Dad and Mom. I sure learned from my dad. For example, when some close friends called him, to his face, a "nigger lover"—there is no good way to say it—because he spoke up for his black brothers and sisters in the Lord, my dad didn't lash out, and he didn't give in. He held his head high and stuck to his principles as a man of God. And I was proud of him. I wanted to be just like him. You, too, can inspire your children by your courageous example. They will be watching.

2. HOSPITALITY

I grew up in a home where all kinds, all colors, and all nations of people were invited in and given a place of honor at our dinner table and a place of comfort in our guest room. I saw Jewish people, African people, Asian people, and many others—even an unwed mother lived with us for six months while she waited for her child to come. No one was so "other" that our door was closed.

Jani and I have tried to establish the same culture of welcome in our own home. When guests come, whatever their color or background or story, Jani rolls out the same "red carpet," with our best food on the dinner table and a fancy basket of snacks and fruits and bottled water in the guest room. Whether they look like us or not, everyone entering our space can know how moved we are that they would trust us with a visit.

And if, in the early church, the Christians greeted one another "with a holy kiss" (2 Corinthians 13:12), then our hospitality can surely include a hug at the front door, an arm around the shoulder on the way in, and an intent gaze into their eyes over dinner with a look deep enough to get past the shallows of social convention.

3. SUFFERING

Good parents shield their children *from* suffering, of course. But wise Christian parents also raise their children *for* suffering. The racism of this world will not surrender easily. The unity of the body of Christ will not prevail easily. If we raise our children to do the right thing, they will suffer along the way. But they don't have to be blindsided. We can prepare them. My own dad taught me from his old King James Bible, "Thou therefore endure hardness, as a good soldier of Jesus Christ" (2 Timothy 2:3). My dad was the most cheerful man I've ever known. But it never entered my mind, growing up as his son, that following Christ would be easy. It *shouldn't* be easy. The gospel is worth everything. Let's impart that vision and that resilience to our children. They're going to need it.

A Prayer for the Next Generation

Please pray with me for the next generation.

Our Father in heaven,
We don't know what to do. We see the evils of racism today. We
see the prejudices of our own hearts, and we don't know what to
do. And so we come to you, the one with all wisdom and power.
We come asking of you, Lord. We ask that your work would be
shown to your servants, and your glorious power to our children.
We ask for your favor, Lord our God, to be upon us. We ask you

to establish the work of our hands. Yes, establish the work of our hands! Father, as we think of our precious children and families, we ask you to build our homes, and that peoples of all nations would be loved in our homes. Lord, we know that if you don't build our homes, we will labor in vain. And so we ask you to build our children up in the knowledge and grace of our Lord Jesus Christ. We ask for you to keep them from racism—that they would be neither victims nor perpetrators of it. And yet Lord, when they feel the sting of racial pain, we pray that you would be near them. And that they would cast themselves wholly upon your grace. Dear God, help us. Hear us. Help our kids. Hear them! Save them, we pray! Equip them to do justice, love mercy, and walk humbly with you. Let them live in a society with less racism and more love. O God, we don't know what to do, but our eyes are on you. We pray in Jesus's name, Amen.

GLOSSARY

Christian. A person who has trusted in Jesus's death and resurrection for salvation by faith alone. While a Christian will not live perfectly in light of this trust, they will live repentantly, in accordance with Scripture.

church, local. A congregation of baptized believers who gather regularly in one place for the administration of the Word and the sacraments of baptism and the Lord's Supper.

church, multiethnic. The general standard of a multiethnic church, established by sociologists (though not mandated by Scripture), is a local church in which one ethnicity does not make up more than 80 percent of the whole congregation.

ethnicity. A word that refers to the way people identify with each other based on commonalties such as language, history, ancestry, nationalities, customs, and values. In the Bible, the Greek word *ethnos* in the New Testament can refer to people groups (who, most basically, would recognize "us" as being different from "them") but can also refer to a nation. In Matthew 28:19 Jesus referred to "all nations" (all *ethnē*).

evangelical. Entire works have been devoted to defining this word. Yet, for my purposes, I simply mean Christians who believe in the authority and inerrancy of Scripture and the gospel message as defined below.

evangelicalism. For the purposes of this book, I use *evangelicalism* to refer to the larger subculture that evangelicals have built around their churches and institutions (schools, publishing houses, music, political involvement, etc.).

gospel. The gospel is the joyous declaration that God is redeeming the world through Christ and that he commands everyone everywhere to turn from sin and trust Jesus Christ for salvation. Each of us has sinned against God, breaking his law and rebelling against his rule, and the penalty for our sin is death and hell. But because of his love, God sent his Son, Jesus, to live, for his people's sake, the perfect, obedient life God requires and to die on the cross in our place for our sin. On the third day, Christ rose bodily from the grave and now reigns in heaven, offering forgiveness, righteousness, resurrection, and eternal blessedness in God's presence to everyone who repents of sin and trusts solely in him for salvation.

race. A word that can refer to "the human race or a specific ethnic group, but which can be falsely used to mean a category of people with an inherently different value than other people."[1] When Scripture speaks of "race," it means group, class, or kind. Biblically, there is one human race, there are many ethnicities, and there are two spiritual races (those in Adam and those in Christ).

race conversation, the. You may hear this phrase often. It is a catch-all term for conversations relating to ethnicity, race, racism, racial justice, racial reconciliation, and so on. The trouble is that the term is so broad that we may be talking about different ideas that overlap but also have important distinctions. Ironically, there is no one "race conversation," thus one person might be having one kind of conversation about race while their listener is desiring another. Hence the frustration we often see.

racial-justice conversation, the. Generally, conversations about racial justice revolve around addressing the injustices different ethnicities, particularly African Americans, have experienced and experience still—both in the church and in broader society. This conversation highlights transgressions that prevent fellowship between believers and other image bearers from flourishing. Racial justice is often emphasized by those in the racial minority. And so, with an eye toward the suffering community, this conversation focuses on Christians loving one another and their neighbor, regardless of the neighbor's religion (Mark 12:31). It focuses on not withholding good to those to whom it is due when it is in our power to do it (Proverbs 3:27). Many Christians appreciate these aims in theory but disagree about how to best carry them out.

racial-reconciliation conversation, the. Generally, conversations about racial reconciliation revolve around Christians of different ethnicities faithfully living in step (in the present) with what Christ has done (in the past) through his death and resurrection: He has made one new, united humanity (Ephesians 2:11–22), a chosen race (1 Peter 2:9). This conversation highlights the importance of unity between believers. Racial reconciliation is often emphasized by those in the racial majority. And so, with an eye toward the church, this conversation focuses on Christians loving one another and building relationships, a goal Christians appreciate. However, many other Christians find this goal, often evoked by calls for unity from the majority, to sound hollow, hypocritical, and out of touch if sins regarding race are not addressed.

racial tragedy. A lamentable event that, regardless of who is right or wrong, echoes or connotes racial tensions and dynamics.

racism. Biblically speaking, racism is ethnic partiality (James 2:1). This partiality can be expressed individually (as we see in Numbers 12 with Aaron and Miriam toward Moses's

Ethiopian wife) or structurally (as we see in Esther, with Haman's state-sponsored initiative to annihilate the Jews); and it can be expressed overtly or covertly.

structural racism. An unjust system (e.g., written or unwritten laws, traditions, procedures, formal or informal habits, cultural practices) that wrongly favors an ethnicity (or race). Structural racism is so insidious because it can operate regardless of one's individual intentions.

ACKNOWLEDGMENTS

Where can I begin? The Zondervan team has been so good to me. Capitol Hill Baptist Church gave me not only time to work but something even greater—hope. And in writing this book, I had no greater need than hope. Why? Because this book isn't just one of the hardest things I've ever written; it's one of the hardest things I've ever done. When writing this book, I often felt like Moses in battle (Exodus 17). *But God* gave me brothers and sisters who kept my hands raised in the fight—my own Aarons and Hurs, whom I can't thank enough. Mark, Matt, Jarvis, Jamie, Jonathan, Bobby, Omar, Collin, Austin, Jeri, Josh—I love you. To those who lent me their stories—I thank you. To Megan, my faithful wife, who never stopped cheering for me—I cherish you. And to the God who had his hands raised and spread for me on the cross—I worship you.

NOTES

Epigraph Page

1. Paul Laurence Dunbar, "We Wear the Mask," Poetry Foundation, www.poetryfoundation.org/poems/44203/we-wear-the-mask.

Why I Wrote This Book

1. Thabiti Anyabwile, "A Call for Hope in the Age of Mass Incarceration," *The Atlantic*, September 15, 2015, www.theatlantic .com/politics/archive/2015/09/why-there-needs-to-be-more-hope /404977/.
2. Sterling K. Brown, Facebook, May 8, 2020, www.facebook.com /925165127600434/posts/2810464472403814/.

Introduction

1. Justin E. Giboney, "Today's Mob Mentality Politics: Just Deny It, and Keep Moving," The Hill, September 6, 2020, https://thehill .com/opinion/campaign/515156-todays-mob-mentality-politics -just-deny-it-and-keep-moving.
2. Martin Luther King Jr., "Letter from a Birmingham Jail," African Studies Center, www.africa.upenn.edu/Articles_Gen/Letter _Birmingham.html.
3. At the risk of this book being a casualty of time, I'm using the term *majority* to refer to white people and *minority* to refer to everyone else. It has been predicted that by 2044, America will be majority minority, and maybe these terms won't make sense then, but we're not there yet.

Part 1

1. Martin Luther King Jr., *Why We Can't Wait*, Signet Classics (New York: Signet, 2000), 68.

Chapter 1: Setting the Scene: A Tragic Shooting, a Viral Video

1. W. E. B. Du Bois, *The Souls of Black Folk* (Mineola, NY: Dover, 1903), v.

Chapter 2: A Majority Mask—Meet Hunter

1. Lance Morrow, "'An Honest Conversation about Race'?" *WSJ*, July 2, 2020, www.wsj.com/articles/an-honest-conversation-about-race-11593728522.

Encouragement for Hunter

1. Alan Jacobs, *How to Think: A Survival Guide for a World at Odds* (New York: Currency, 2017), 68.
2. For more on why many white brothers and sisters tend to individualize race problems, see Michael O. Emerson and Christian Smith, "Color Blind: Evangelicals Speak on the 'Race Problem,'" in Emerson and Smith, *Divided by Faith: Evangelical Religion and the Problem of Race in America* (New York: Oxford University Press, 2001).
3. I'm indebted to Alex Medina for this probing question.
4. James Baldwin, *Nobody Knows My Name* (1954; repr., New York: Vintage, 1993), 106–7.
5. Here's an example of an exception: When it comes to speaking on segregation, who should speak first, me or Douglas Massey, coauthor of *American Apartheid: Segregation and the Making of the Underclass*, who looks as white as people come? Probably Massey, because he is an expert on the topic. One doesn't even have to be an expert to speak, either. Indeed, the better your friendship is with someone, the more freedom you'll have to speak. And yet, from my experience, I know of no friendship so close that personal backgrounds can be ignored altogether. In fact, the better friend you are to someone, the more you'll likely seek to consider your friend's background more, not less, as you seek to love them.

Chapter 3: A Minority Mask—Meet Darius

1. Isaac Chotiner, "Bryan Stevenson on the Frustration behind the George Floyd Protests," *New Yorker*, June 1, 2020, www.newyorker .com/news/q-and-a/bryan-stevenson-on-the-frustration-behind -the-george-floyd-protests.

Encouragement for Darius

1. Jackie Hill Perry, "Merciful Mouths: Bold and Foolish Words," United? We Pray (podcast), November 15, 2017, https://uwepray .com/feed/0105.

2. Campbell Robertson, "A Quiet Exodus: Why Black Worshipers Are Leaving White Evangelical Churches," *New York Times*, March 9, 2018, www.nytimes.com/2018/03/09/us/blacks- evangelical-churches.html. "Black Exodus" refers to a trend of black believers leaving predominantly white churches after the 2016 presidential election. This exodus continued during the 2020 election. See Sarah Pulliam Bailey, "Black and White Evangelicals Once Talked about 'Racial Reconciliation.' Then Trump Came Along," August 21, 2020, *Washington Post*, www.washingtonpost .com/religion/2020/08/21/black-and-white-evangelicals-trump -racial-reconciliation/.

3. For more on what some minorities wish they heard in predominantly white churches, see Gerado Marti and Michael O. Emerson's seminal essay "The Rise of the Diversity Expert: How American Evangelicals Simultaneously Accentuate and Ignore Race," in *The New Evangelical Social Engagement*, ed. Brian Steensland and Philip Goff (New York: Oxford University Press, 2014).

4. I am grateful to Thabiti Anyabwile for this point.

5. I am grateful to Mike Kelsey for giving me words to summarize Darius's work.

6. I'm indebted to Irwyn Ince for this point about ethnic identity no longer being *the* thing about us. Irwyn Ince, "A Crown of Beauty in the Hand of the Lord," byFaith, October 1, 2020, https://byfaithonline.com/a-crown-beauty-hand-of-lord -community-irwyn-ince/.

7. Howard Thurman, *Jesus and the Disinherited* (Boston: Beacon, 1996), 68.

Chapter 4: A Majority Mask—Meet Anna Beth and Samantha Lee

1. Emma Green, "The Unofficial Racism Consultants to the White Evangelical World," *The Atlantic*, July 5, 2020, www.theatlantic.com/politics/archive/2020/07/white-evangelicals-black-lives-matter/613738/.

Encouragement for Anna Beth

1. Robert P. George and Cornel West, "To Unite the Country, We Need Honesty and Courage," *Boston Globe*, July 15, 2020, www.bostonglobe.com/2020/07/15/opinion/unite-country-we-need-honesty-courage/.

2. I make this distinction about physical differences because often when we think about diversity, we look for people who look physically different from us but who are culturally the same. And if we're not careful, this can tend toward tokenism. (I'm indebted to Pastor Jerome Gay for this point about tokenism.) It's this kind of tokenism that leads white brothers and sisters to say, "But my black friend says this!" I'm not saying that a friend who doesn't look like you but shares your social intuitions or political sympathies is a bad friend to have or, in this example, that they're not "really black." I'm simply saying that you shouldn't use that one friend to justify your views about the world or about an ethnic group in it; you shouldn't use that friend to affirm your inaction toward your neighbor.

3. For more on catalytic events, see Brenda Salter McNeil, "Shake it Up! The Power of Catalytic Events," in McNeil, *Roadmap to Reconciliation: Moving Communities into Unity, Wholeness and Justice* (Downers Grove, IL: InterVarsity, 2015). McNeil helpfully states the power of catalytic events in our lives: "Many of us are interested in talking about strategies for reconciliation, and that's good. But we need to realize that the most powerful ways we change are often out of our control. Change can be painful and coercive because we cannot control or manage it. . . . Comprehensive change is arduous,

difficult and often *very* slow, because it requires us to give up long-held beliefs and assumptions. That's why it often takes a catalytic event in our lives to *force* us out of our spaces of comfort and into new spaces of growth and transformation" (emphasis original) (p. 46).

4. John McWhorter, "The Great Awokening: Atonement as Activism," *The American Interest* 14.1 (May 24, 2018), www.the -american-interest.com/2018/05/24/atonement-as-activism/.

Encouragement for Samantha Lee

1. Robert P. George and Cornel West, "To Unite the Country, We Need Honesty and Courage," *Boston Globe*, July 15, 2020, https:// www.bostonglobe.com/2020/07/15/opinion/unite-country -we-need-honesty-courage/.

2. Martin Luther King Jr., "I Have a Dream: Full Text March on Washington Speech," NAACP, www.naacp.org/i-have-a-dream -speech-full-march-on-washington/.

3. George Yancey, *Beyond Racial Gridlock: Embracing Mutual Responsibility* (Downers Grove, IL: InterVarsity, 2006), 31.

4. In their book *Divided by Faith*, Michael Emerson and Christian Smith teach about the useful concept of racialization—that is, living in a society in which race matters "profoundly for differences in life experiences, life opportunities, and social relationships," regardless of personal feelings. Michael O. Emerson and Christian Smith, *Divided by Faith: Evangelical Religion and the Problem of Race in America* (New York: Oxford University Press, 2001), 7.

5. Esau McCaulley, *Reading While Black: African American Biblical Interpretation as an Exercise in Hope* (Downers Grove, IL: IVP Academic, 2020), 114.

6. McCaulley, *Reading While Black*, 114.

7. For more on why color blindness is not supported by Galatians 3:28, see Jarvis Williams, "Galatians 3:28 Does Not Encourage Color-Blind Christianity," The Witness, June 2, 2016, https:// thewitnessbcc.com/galatians-328-not-encourage-color-blind -christianity/.

8. For more on this interpretation of King's "I Have a Dream" speech, see McCaulley, *Reading While Black*, 112–13.

9. C. Herbert Oliver, *No Flesh Shall Glory: How the Bible Destroys the Foundations of Racism*, 2nd ed. (Phillipsburg, NJ: P&R, 2021), 19.

10. David P. Leong, *Race and Place: How Urban Geography Shapes the Journey to Reconciliation* (Downers Grove, IL: InterVarsity, 2017), 41.

11. Some brothers and sisters may be uncomfortable with words like *systemic*. Jim Crow laws are one example of what I'm talking about when I say "systemic." The Southern Baptist Convention (SBC) didn't shy from speaking of systemic racism in their 1995 resolution, given on June 1, 1995, the 150th anniversary of the SBC: "Be it further RESOLVED, That we apologize to all African-Americans for condoning and/or perpetuating individual and systemic racism in our lifetime; and we genuinely repent of racism of which we have been guilty, whether consciously (Psalm 19:13) or unconsciously (Leviticus 4:27)" ("Resolution on Racial Reconciliation on the 150th Anniversary of the Southern Baptist Convention," www.sbc.net/resource-library/resolutions/resolution -on-racial-reconciliation-on-the-150th-anniversary-of-the -southern-baptist-convention/).

12. Alexis McGill Johnson, "I'm the Head of Planned Parenthood. We're Done Making Excuses for Our Founder," *New York Times*, April 17, 2021, www.nytimes.com/2021/04/17/opinion/planned-parenthood -margaret-sanger.html. Ms. McGill Johnson is the president and chief executive of the Planned Parenthood Federation of America.

13. J. I. Packer, *"Fundamentalism" and the Word of God* (Grand Rapids: Eerdmans, 1958), 35.

14. Os Guinness, *Fit Bodies, Fat Minds: Why Evangelicals Don't Think and What to Do about It* (Grand Rapids: Baker, 1994), 144. Guinness reflects on the danger of thinking there is one Christian way to think about everything. This misconception of uniformity, what Guinness calls particularism, "is disastrous because it leads inevitably to legalism and judgmentalism. There is only one short and easy step from 'This is the Christian way' to 'There is only one Christian way' to 'Anything different from this way is not

Christian' to 'All those who differ from my way are not Christians.' Far too many a letter from one Christian to another has begun in reality or in spirit, 'Dear former brother/sister in Christ.' The fallacy of particularism stems from the fact that God has not spoken definitively to us about everything" (144–45).

Chapter 5: A Minority Mask—Meet Jane (Eun-ji)

1. "What about the Other 'Other'? More Than a Black/White Conversation (w/Duke Kwon)," United? We Pray (podcast), May 23, 2018, https://uwepray.com/feed/0207.

Encouragement for Jane

1. "Being Asian American in a White Church," 9Marks, accessed March 7, 2021, https://www.9marks.org/article/being-asian -american-in-a-white-church/. Tim's insights from this article, some of which appear in this chapter, were massively helpful to me.
2. Steve S. Chang, "Why Asian Americans Struggle to Feel at Home in White-Majority Churches," TGC, November 16, 2017, https:// www.thegospelcoalition.org/article/asian-americans-struggle-feel -home-white-majority-churches/.
3. Two resources on the biblical practice of lament are Soong-Chan Rah, *Prophetic Lament: A Call for Justice in Troubled Times* (Downers Grove, IL: InterVarsity Press, 2015); and Mark Vroegop, *Weep with Me: How Lament Opens a Door for Racial Reconciliation* (Wheaton, IL: Crossway, 2020).
4. "How often the church has been an echo rather than a voice, a taillight behind the Supreme Court and other agencies, rather than a headlight guiding men progressively and decisively into higher levels of understanding." Martin Luther King Jr., *Strength to Love* (Minneapolis: Fortress, 2010), 105. In a sobering indictment about how American churches had failed to lead against racism, theologian C. Hebert Oliver suggested that "Christians seem to learn more slowly than the children of darkness, for the world seems to be leading the way in the battle against the dogmas of racism" (*No Flesh Shall Glory*, 21).

Chapter 6: A Man among Masks—Meet Their Pastor

1. Jonathan Leeman (@JonathanLeeman), Twitter, November 16, 2019, 11:09 a.m., https://twitter.com/JonathanLeeman/status /1195735369335156736.

Encouragement for Their Pastor

1. I'm grateful to Cameron Triggs for this pastoral exhortation.
2. "James Baldwin: The Price of a Ticket," *American Masters*, PBS, rebroadcast August 23, 2013, http://to.pbs.org/17eSKUJ.
3. John Piper, "Racial Diversity in Hell," desiringGod.org, April 1, 2009, https://www.desiringgod.org/articles/racial-diversity-in-hell.
4. For this method of theological triage, I'm drawing upon Andrew David Naselli and J. D. Crowley, *Conscience: What It Is, How to Train It, and Loving Those Who Differ* (Wheaton, IL: Crossway, 2016), 86–87.
5. In his article, pastor Jamie Dunlop highlights the cost of what so many of us say we want in our churches—diversity. Dunlop goes on to say, "Pastors should address important, secondary issues from the pulpit. But if your church is composed of a diversity of perspectives on these issues—because you're united around Christ alone—then your pastor's statements will be less focused, less frequent, and less forceful than anyone would prefer—including him. And as Christians, love overruns preference" (Jamie Dunlop, "Diversity Is Costly," United? We Pray, February 2, 2021, https:// uwepray.com/articles/diversity-costly).
6. Martin Luther King Jr., "Letter from a Birmingham Jail," African Studies Center, www.africa.upenn.edu/Articles_Gen/Letter _Birmingham.html.
7. Of course, the church scattered (i.e., individuals members of the church) will carry out mercy and justice in lots of different ways, but the church gathered (i.e., the corporate body) is more limited in what it does, as not all the members need be bound to the same course of action if Scripture doesn't prescribe it.

Part 2

1. Martin Luther King Jr., *Why We Can't Wait*, Signet Classics (New York: Signet, 2000), 68.

Chapter 7: Why Should We Talk about Race across Color Lines?

1. Mark said this quote to me in a conversation, though it draws on comments from his T4G 2012 address (Mark Dever, "False Conversions: The Suicide of the Church [Session III]," T4G, https://t4g.org/resources/mark-dever/false-conversions-the -suicide-of-the-church-2/).

2. Richard Baxter, *The Cure of Church-Divisions, or Directions for Weak Christians, to Keep Them from Being Dividers, or Troublers of the Church: With Some Directions to . . . Deal with Such Christians* (1670; repr., London: Forgotten Books, 2018). The three questions listed about zeal are from Baxter.

3. Francis Schaeffer, "The Mark of a Christian," accessed March 7, 2021, https://static1.squarespace.com/static/5a63ca49a803bbb2281732b1/t /5a999369419202db743a69bb/1520014185180/%E2%80%9CThe +Mark+of+the+Christian%E2%80%9D+by+Francis+Schaeffer.pdf.

4. I praise God that there were white Christians who stood on the right side of racial justice. Yet the point I'm highlighting and wrestling with here is why so many didn't.

5. I can't articulate this point about the demonic nature of racism any better than my sister in Christ (and in blood) Hannah Adams, who remarked, "I believe racism is a principality of the kingdom of darkness, and Satan has used it for generations to divide and destroy, to make Christians less effective in drawing others to Christ."

6. James Baldwin commented on how racist ideologies pervert the minds of those who hold them. He said, "I suggest that what has happened to the white Southerner is in some ways much worse than what has happened to Negroes there" (James Baldwin, "The American Dream and the American Negro," *New York Times*, March 7, 1965, https://archive.nytimes.com/www.nytimes.com /books/98/03/29/specials/baldwin-dream.html?_r=1&oref=slogin.

7. Charles Marsh, *God's Long Summer: Stories of Faith and Civil Rights* (1997; repr., Princeton, NJ: Princeton University Press, 2008), 22–23.

Chapter 8: Why Is It So Hard to Talk about Race across Color Lines?

1. David French, "American Racism: We've Got So Very Far to Go," The Dispatch, June 7, 2020, https://frenchpress.thedispatch.com /p/american-racism-weve-got-so-very.

2. Kevin DeYoung, "Racial Reconciliation: What We (Mostly, Almost) All Agree On, and What We (Likely) Still Don't Agree On," TGC, April 17, 2018, www.thegospelcoalition.org/blogs/ kevin-deyoung/racial-reconciliation-mostly-almost-agree-likely -still-dont-agree/.

3. Esau McCaulley, *Reading While Black: African American Biblical Interpretation as an Exercise in Hope* (Downers Grove, IL: IVP Academic, 2020), 131.

4. This section draws heavily upon Austin Suter's fine piece, "White People Often Engage Racism As an Idea, Not an Experience," United? We Pray, August 11, 2020, https://uwepray.com/articles/ united-we-pray-racism-as-idea-or-experience.

5. I'm not saying that white brothers or sisters haven't been on the receiving end of racism that was evil. But as we considered in Hunter's chapter, asymmetry probably makes it so that a white brother or sister doesn't feel that racism as a minority would.

6. "Lincoln's Second Inaugural Address," National Park Service, www.nps.gov/linc/learn/historyculture/lincoln-second-inaugural .htm.

7. Matt Merker (@MerkerMatt), Twitter, September 29, 2020, 12:44 p.m., https://twitter.com/MerkerMatt/status/1310983903998611460.

8. Mark DeYmaz, "New Research on Multiethnic Churches, *Outreach Magazine*, March 29, 2020, https://outreachmagazine.com/features /multiethnic/53748-new-research-on-multiethnic-churches.html.

9. Jemar Tisby, *The Color of Compromise: The Truth about the American Church's Complicity in Racism* (Grand Rapids: Zondervan, 2019), 52–54.

10. Tom Gjelten, "Multiracial Congregations May Not Bridge Racial

Divide," NPR, July 17, 2020, https://www.npr.org/2020/07/17/891600067/multiracial-congregations-may-not-bridge-racial-divide.

11. On one level, we can understand why minorities attend white churches at a higher rate than whites attend minority churches. Minorities are used to operating within the majority culture, whereas whites are typically not used to operating in minority cultures. It's like English being one of the major trade languages in places that aren't England. You can generally count on people speaking it, and people are used to speaking it. So, someone who doesn't have great English may very well land in an English-speaking church. It's rarer, however, and much more difficult, for an English speaker to go to a non-English speaking church. But in my opinion, this fact—that it is in some sense stranger for whites to attend minority churches— gives white brothers and sisters that much more of an opportunity to display gospel unity. It makes worldly sense, on some level, that minorities would flow into a predominantly white church (though with the history of slavery, this is still a supernatural feat!). It doesn't make as much sense for that flow to go the opposite way. And that's one sweet thing the gospel does—it leads us to do things that don't make worldly sense. I know white brothers and sisters can be timid about appearing as colonizers when it comes to thinking about going to a non-white church. Get over that fear. Don't go as a colonizer. Go as a Christian and love your family in Christ.

12. I'm grateful to Nick Rodriguez for this insight about either forbidding conversations or lowering the temperature within them.

13. Os Guinness, *Fit Bodies, Fat Minds: Why Evangelicals Don't Think and What to Do about It* (Grand Rapids: Baker, 1994), 42.

14. C. Herbert Oliver, *No Flesh Shall Glory: How the Bible Destroys the Foundations of Racism*, 2nd ed. (Phillipsburg, NJ: P&R, 2021), 70.

Chapter 9: How Should We Talk about Race across Color Lines?

1. Many thanks to Keith Plummer for his constant, hope-giving friendship to me, as shown in these words.

2. J. I. Packer, *"Fundamentalism" and the Word of God* (Grand Rapids: Eerdmans, 1958), 19.

3. John Onwuchekwa, *Prayer: How Praying Together Shapes the Church*, 9Marks: Building Healthy Churches (Wheaton, IL: Crossway, 2018), 101–2.

4. Francis Grimké, *The Negro: His Rights and Wrongs, the Forces for Him and Against Him* (Cornell University Library, 1898), 80–81, 85.

Chapter 10: Closing the Scene: Forgiveness

1. Elaina Plott, "Her Facebook Friends Asked If Anyone Was Actually Sick. She Had an Answer," *New York Times*, March 19, 2020, https://www.nytimes.com/2020/03/19/us/politics/coronavirus-heaven-frilot-mark-frilot.html.

Chapter 11: When the Next Racial Tragedy Happens, What Can You Do?

1. I am indebted to Rich Villodas for this point.

Afterword: Little Masks—Talking about Race with Your Kids

1. Martin Luther King Jr., "I Have a Dream: Full Text March on Washington Speech," NAACP, www.naacp.org/i-have-a-dream-speech-full-march-on-washington/.

Glossary

1. Curtis A. Woods and Jarvis J. Williams, *The Gospel in Color for Parents: A Theology of Racial Reconciliation for Parents* (Vancouver, WA: Patrol, 2018), 42.

SCRIPTURE INDEX

UNITED?
we pray

It is a serious matter . . . when any body of people, however few, betake themselves not to revolt but to prayer.

—REV. FRANCIS GRIMKÉ, 1898

Taking racial struggles to the throne of grace, United? We Pray is a ministry devoted to prayer about racial strife—especially between Christians. We want to help Christians think better about race in a way that is biblical and helpful, clear and hopeful.

Learn more about our work at uwepray.com.